WE ARE THE OCEAN

We Are the Ocean

Selected Works

Epeli Hau‘ofa

University of Hawai‘i Press
Honolulu

Printed in the United States of America
21 20 19 8 7 6

LIBRARY OF CONGRESS CATALOGING-IN-PUBLICATION DATA

Hau'ofa, Epeli.
We are the ocean : selected works / Epeli Hauofa.
p. cm.
ISBN 978-0-8248-3173-8 (pbk. : alk. paper)
I. Title.
PR9655.9.H38A6 2008
823—dc22
2007036652

University of Hawai'i Press books are printed on acid-free paper and meet the guidelines for permanence and durability of the Council on Library Resources.

Designed by University of Hawai'i Press production staff

For Barbara

Contents

Foreword by Geoffrey White ix
Preface xxi

Part I: Rethinking

- Anthropology and Pacific Islanders 3
- The New South Pacific Society: Integration and Independence 11

Part II: Reflecting

- Our Sea of Islands 27
- The Ocean in Us 41
- Pasts to Remember 60
- Our Place Within: Foundations for a Creative Oceania 80

Part III: Creating

- The Writer as an Outsider 97
- The Glorious Pacific Way 110
- The Tuktuks (Excerpt from *Kisses in the Nederends*) 120
- Oilei and Babu (Excerpt from *Kisses in the Nederends*) 125
- Epeli Hau'ofa Interviewed by Subramani 136

Part IV: Revisiting

- Thy Kingdom Come: The Democratisation of Aristocratic Tonga 157
- His Majesty King Tāufa'āhau Tupou IV: An Appreciation 172
- Blood in the Kava Bowl 180

Index 183

Foreword

Geoffrey White

Many readers who come to this volume will need no introduction to the essays that follow. This is fortunate since Epeli Hau'ofa's writings have traversed so many spaces in Oceania that any attempt to introduce them is condemned to partiality if not triviality. That said, it is with ambivalent gratitude that I acknowledge Epeli's invitation to provide a few prefatory notes.

In 2003 Epeli gave a series of invited talks at the University of Hawai'i and the East-West Center. Everyone in attendance knew that he was at it again; stirring things up with a new project: the Oceania Centre for Arts and Culture. Provoked by the quiet excitement of that occasion, a group of friends and colleagues began to discuss the need for a collection of Epeli's writings. There was never a question of why. By that time he had already authored numerous essays and works of fiction that were reverberating through the region, affecting the ways people think and talk about the Pacific, including the ways scholars engage with Oceania through their writing and teaching. This collection brings together some of the key works from his career as ethnographer, satirist, professor, artist, farmer, and clown.

Given the range of Epeli's writing, it was clear from the start that a volume of collected works would bring together a unique combination of styles and genres. True to form, this volume includes analytic articles, cultural essays, interviews, a short story (from *Tales of the Tikongs*), two excerpts from longer fiction *(Kisses in the Nederends),* and poetry as well as artwork from members of the Oceania Centre for Arts and Culture. The table of contents makes a stab at ordering this unlikely conjunction, grouping together earlier analytic works, cultural criticism, fiction and confessional pieces, and—reminding us of the author's abiding attachment to his ancestral homeland—an essay, a eulogy, and a poem on Tongan society and culture.

Behind the diversity of writing gathered here is a life story marked by commitment and creativity. As is often the case with influential artists and intellectuals, Epeli has kept exploring new styles and approaches, all the while sustained by a deep sense of Oceanian values. As he moved between his island homeland(s) and more arid academic circles, he developed a keen sense of the uncanny—the contradictions that mark points of intersection between these worlds. Using a variety of disciplinary practices, from the ethnographer's eye to the satirist's pen, he manages to disturb conventional realities and illuminate what is at stake in Oceania and in the world today.

Certain junctures in Epeli's life story are well known. They are repeated often as he is introduced as a keynote speaker or contributing author. He is frequently described as someone who has progressed from social research (PhD in anthropology) to fiction and art. In this respect Epeli's personal story is also a collective story—a kind of parable for the postcolonial Pacific. As evinced through the writings gathered here, his work punctuates the brief history of Pacific studies, beginning in the early moments of independence for South Pacific nations and wending its way through paradigms of decolonization, "development," and globalization. Just as linear narratives of progress through economic modernization have come unhinged in today's globalized Pacific, Epeli's voice has always been capable of disrupting dogma and bringing fresh air to the often-suffocating seriousness of convention. In doing so he offers Pacific Islanders a place to breathe, a vantage point from which to imagine a new Pacific. Along the way his writing, speaking, and performing have been a lightning rod for conversation and debate. Consider the historical context for Epeli's work.

After a BA in history at the University of New England (1965), Epeli undertook graduate studies in anthropology at McGill University (MA, 1968) and Australian National University (PhD, 1975) at the very time that the first South Pacific states were obtaining their independence (Fiji 1970; Papua New Guinea 1975; Solomon Islands 1978; Vanuatu 1980). By that time he had developed an Oceanian sensibility as a Tongan born and raised in Papua New Guinea (Milne Bay). By the age of nine he had already lived in three Papua New Guinea societies, including a formative period in Misima during World War II, as well as brief periods in Australia and Tonga. Well before the surge in regional circulation that would create a diasporic Pacific, he learned to speak seven Pacific languages, including English.

It was perhaps inevitable that Epeli, having grown up in the colonial era, would be drawn into anthropology—the field of Western scholarship most entangled with Pacific societies during that period. He first went to

McGill University to study sociology but, unmoved by that subject, shifted to anthropology, ultimately completing a master's degree that included fieldwork in Trinidad where he discovered V. S. Naipaul, whose early writings were an important influence in his development as a humorist and satirist. For his PhD work in anthropology, Epeli returned to the Pacific, studying at ANU and carrying out research in Papua New Guinea. From that work he produced a major book about the Mekeo (*Mekeo: Inequality and Ambivalence in a Village Society,* ANU Press, 1981), a lasting contribution despite its relative absence from lists that emphasize Epeli's creative writing. While quite different from his later work, a close reading of *Mekeo* shows that he was already pushing the limits of ethnographic writing in order to create more human forms of representation.

Even as Epeli was completing his dissertation at ANU, he addressed his discomfort with disciplinary conventions in an article titled "Anthropology and Pacific Islanders." That essay, given to an ANZAAS conference in Canberra in 1975 and published in the journal *Oceania,* is the earliest of his essays included here. Written in the pithy style characteristic of much of his later writing, it foreshadowed issues that were just beginning to unsettle the field of anthropology and would be a major theme in decades to come. As one of the first native Pacific Islanders entering a field renowned for its ability to produce "expert" knowledge about Pacific peoples, Epeli confronted the contradictions experienced by those who found their own subjectivity caught up in the webs of an objectifying science practiced by others. He has done so with humor and (self) parody, as well as incisive critical essays. Although the term was not yet in general usage, his 1975 reflection anticipated elements of Edward Said's influential book *Orientalism.* His concerns about the depersonalizing effects of conventional ethnographic writing set the stage for later work critiquing academic discourses that reproduce many of the same imbalances of power and agency associated with colonial history.

The sentiments of skepticism evident in that paper would work themselves out in other ways as Epeli returned to his ancestral home, Tonga, for about five years as a research fellow, a "dropout and failed poet," and a civil servant and two years as an employee of the University of the South Pacific. That period of his life proved to be one of intense creativity fueled by his sense of alienation from the Tongan establishment. In that period he wrote three books and a good deal of poetry and in the process realized his own proclivity for fiction. He wrote his first short story (the first of the *Tales*) just after he had completed revising his dissertation for publication and was engaged in writing a "very dry report" on a long-running research project. Whereas those projects proved to be "arduous and almost soul-destroying exercises," writing his first tale was such a "refreshing experience" that he began to shift the locus of his writing ("The Writer as an Outsider").

While in Tonga, Epeli was recruited by the University of the South Pacific to be the foundation director of its new Rural Development Centre there. As the major regional university and hub for social and economic research in the Pacific, the Suva-based University of the South Pacific has always been deeply involved in the practical machinery of Pacific "development." In Epeli's case, he was already in demand as a consultant and asked to advise about pressing problems following in the wake of independence. Unlike others, however, he could not settle easily into the role of native consultant—or at least not without a measure of satire. He has characterized this period of his life:

> As one of the two resident natives with PhD degrees, I found my views and opinions on a wide range of issues much sought after by local residents as well as by an endless stream of visiting experts, advisers, academics, postgraduate students, journalists, some ordinary tourists, and even a few international crooks and wheeler-dealers. It did not seem to matter to others that my views and opinions on most matters were decidedly ill informed; I dished them out freely. . . . ["The Writer as an Outsider"]

In his essay "The New South Pacific Society," published in the edited volume *Class and Culture in the South Pacific* (1987), Epeli analyzed the process of decolonization as one that involved increasing integration of Pacific societies into the global economy and its regional centers in Australia and New Zealand (and, presumably today, Asia). As part of this process, he observed the emergence of class distinctions and structural inequalities associated with postcolonial development. Presciently he worried that these problems were often overlooked in simplistic discussions of the opposition of tradition and modernity. Here cultural tradition is anything but romantic. "It is the poor who have to live out the traditional culture; the privileged can merely talk about it." Noting the divergence of interests between ordinary islanders and Pacific elites connected with the engines of global capital (and the disbursement of aid money), Epeli alerted his readers to the socioeconomic consequences of globalization in the Pacific long before the term became fashionable.

Looking ahead to the work that would follow, "The New South Pacific Society" held the seeds of an approach that would ultimately focus on the force of imagination. Here "development"—the central trope defining relations between the indigenous Pacific and global capitalism—is not only a process of economic change. It is a way of thinking, a discourse that creates its own reality. Looking back on the 1960s and 1970s, Epeli recalls that, with the drive for development, "suddenly our world changed; we were poor." In other words, "development" creates "poverty" even in societies that may be largely self-sufficient outside the cash economy. "Development" in this view is a way of thinking about oneself and the wider world. As concerns with poverty and "underdevelopment" become internalized, dependency theory becomes, in Marshall Sahlins' words, "despondency theory." Here political economy is as much a politics of perspective and epistemology as anything else. In this light, the tools of the writer, especially humor and parody, suddenly become relevant, just as the clown can joke about the powerful who otherwise remain circumscribed by protocols of respect. No wonder that the tales Epeli began to tell during his sojourn in Tonga would provide the means for his reply to the forces of development.

Tales of the Tikongs, a gem of a book, may be the most insightful thing ever written about the culture of "development" in the Pacific. Each story about life among the Tikongs portrays some aspect of the subtle distortions and absurdities that emerge in the borderzones between island cultures and global economic forces. The beauty of these tales is that each captures just enough of the familiar, mundane detail of daily life to render plausible stories that descend quickly into the absurd. The story included here, "The Glorious Pacific Way," conjures up a scenario in which Ole Pasifikiwei, a low-level government functionary and part-time recorder of oral traditions, finds a connection with a government ministry and a foreign diplomat eager to dispense financial assistance. ("We have money set aside for the promotion of culture preservation projects in the Pacific.") Ole quickly learns his role in the aid machine. Overcoming his shame about asking for a typewriter and filing cabinet, he thinks: "It's like committing sin: once you start it becomes progressively easier." And indeed it does. By the end of the story, six years later, our hero Ole has applied for a total of $14 million for his small empire of cultural preservation and has been awarded an honorary doctoral degree from the University of the Southern Paradise. Epeli's reflections about his own experiences in this Neverland indicate that his tales are indeed drawn to some degree from personal experience.

In discussing his thinking on these issues with a group of college teachers assembled at the East-West Center in 2003, Epeli recalled his experience with a neighbor in Tonga who embodied some of the virtues of "crazy" perspectives on the normal. Upon arriving in Tonga in 1975, Epeli encountered an individual regarded as crazy because, among other aberrations, he defied Tongan norms of hierarchy and respect. Epeli remembers this person asserting: "You know, Epeli, I'm the freest person in Tonga. People think I'm crazy so I can say whatever I want." In addition to criticizing the powerful in Tonga, this person also decried the ways in which European powers had shrunk the world of Islanders, especially by restricting travel between Polynesian islands—say between Tonga, Samoa, Uvea, and so on. "We've lost our relatives and they have lost us. We are all lost relatives." Epeli remembers becoming aware for the first time of the way in which "colonialism had isolated us, . . . diverted us from *our* connections, from our traditional connections and redirected our connections to themselves. . . . That's the beginning of belittlement."

Epeli has referred to his work from the early 1990s onward as Project New Oceania. In his view, that project begins with the article "Our Sea of Islands," published in 1993. That article, written in Hilo, Hawai'i, for an invited lecture to an academic group in Pacific studies, flowed in a single rush of writing. As he recalls, he "wrote it one morning, took all day to write, and then delivered it in the evening as a lecture." This is visionary stuff; the kind of literary production that flows from experience and emotion—evident in the essay's personal tone lamenting the predicament of island students caught up in academic practices that continually decenter one's own sense of self. "Our Sea of Islands," as Epeli puts it, was written "with an aim of exorcising a particularly nasty ghost, the ghost of belittlement."

In conjuring up (and exorcising) the ghosts of belittlement, Epeli speaks in a confessional voice. He notes his own complicity in propagating academic visions of Oceania as "peoples of tiny isolated resource-less island states and territories, condemned to dependency on the largesse of powerful countries." But if his professional experience has been entangled in that dominant view, he also draws on his personal experience living in Oceania to construct an alternative. Harking back to his childhood in Papua New

Guinea, he recalls that "we never thought of ourselves as being from small places. We spent most of our time by the sea [where we] could see this vast ocean and knew there were other places beyond, where our friends or relatives were." Growing up in Papua New Guinea, in the Milne Bay area made famous by Bronislaw Malinowski and his account of the vast circuits of *kula* exchange, he would witness the elaborate exchange systems involving highly prized shell valuables and impressive voyaging canoes. He remembers watching the huge seagoing double-hulled canoes, "fantastically designed and decorated," sailing by or bringing traders ashore. With this experience (and of course the Pacific War raging overhead and over the horizon), his childhood world was not small. And despite the absence of electricity and motor vehicles, neither was his world impoverished.

Echoing his "crazy" Tongan neighbor, Epeli came to see a past where people traveled unhindered by newly drawn boundaries. In this vision, the whole of Oceania is connected. Neighboring communities have always exchanged ideas and products—often across vast distances like links in a chain, across the ocean or between shore and mountainous interior. Along these routes of interconnection, both people and things have traveled. Epeli's vision is informed by experience in Papua New Guinea where shells from coastal islands would find their way through the island chain and all the way up to the highlands, hundreds of miles across mountains, to remote areas of the interior.

Given this vivid early experience with an Oceania in which the sea was more of a highway between places than a barrier, Epeli inevitably chafed against the Eurocentric view of islands as remote, isolated, and dependent. Casting his ethnographer's eye on these Europeans arriving from large continental homelands, he diagnoses a failure of vision and understanding that underpins the operation of colonial power. With little comprehension of Oceanian cultures or people, these new arrivals saw only small islands far removed from the large landmasses of Europe.

While some might characterize the vision in "Our Sea of Islands" as hopelessly nostalgic, Epeli is quick to locate his vision in the contemporary Pacific. He might confess to the charge of romanticism, but he is certainly not looking backward. In today's Pacific diaspora he sees the same spirit of exploration, exchange, and expansion that prevailed among the Polynesians who used voyaging canoes to settle oceanic islands that, taken all together, would become the largest cultural nation on earth. (The Polynesian language family stretches from Aotearoa New Zealand to Hawai'i and Rapa Nui.) Today Pacific Islanders routinely transit thousands of miles to trade in commodities that sustain cultural practices linking Oceanian populations spanning island homelands and metropolitan centers around the Pacific Rim. Examples are not hard to find. In "Our Sea of Islands" Epeli tells the story of a Tongan friend living in Berkeley, California, who regularly travels to Fiji and returns with thousands of dollars worth of kava for sale to Polynesian communities in California. And on one occasion when I greeted Epeli arriving at Honolulu International Airport, he emerged from customs carrying a large package for a Tongan lady he had met in transit. He was traveling light and so agreed to help her with her baggage. As it turned out, he was assisting with the circulation of Tongan tapa cloth, produced in Tonga but headed for Honolulu or California where it would be used for ceremonial occasions.

As recounted in the essay "Our Place Within," Epeli's work has moved from fiction and essay writing to more active means for challenging the mindset of belittlement. Seeing artistic production as a powerful vehicle for expressing visions of Oceania, Epeli has in recent years put his energy into creating a space for artistic production in all its aspects—the Oceania Centre for Arts and Culture on the campus of the University of the South Pacific. As Epeli tells the origin story of the Oceania Centre, it springs from the need for alternatives to development models that emanate from elsewhere. In 1992 the governing council of USP resolved to create a program in Pacific arts and culture modeled on the Polynesian Cultural Center (PCC) in Hawai'i—Hawai'i's leading tourist attraction which is managed by the Mormon Church in association with the church-run Brigham Young University. Administrators wished to create a new PCC-style center in Suva, but the faculty of USP disagreed, saying that the university should not turn culture and arts into touristic entertainment. Much of the ensuing debate revolved around ambivalent views of what is "contemporary" and the relative worth of *teaching* art as opposed to *doing* art. In 1997, after some years of delay, Epeli was appointed director of a new center that would be a locus for artistic work expressing local Oceanian styles and sensibilities.

Epeli acknowledges two major influences on his thinking about the shape and direction of the new center. First was the work of Ulli Beier and Georgina Beier at the University of Papua New Guinea and the Institute of Papua New Guinea Studies in Port Moresby in the 1960s and 1970s. Second was the 'Atenisi Institute created by his friend and colleague Futa Helu in Tonga. Epeli notes that the Beiers were invited by USP to advise the university on its project by drawing on their experience in Papua New Guinea and earlier work in Nigeria. Epeli recalls particularly the approach of Georgina Beier who, with her own working-class background in Britain, had no inhibitions about recruiting artists from the ranks of illiterate laborers and remote areas of PNG. In the case of the 'Atenisi Institute, Epeli looked in admiration at the ability of the Tongan scholar and educator Futa Helu to build a university in Tonga with only meager support. The lack of resources did not prevent him from creating an institution based on Socratic methods of inquiry and dialogue—and with a curriculum that included the classics of both Tonga and the West.

The Oceania Centre for Arts and Culture, according to Epeli's brief genealogy, is built more on vision and imagination than on the physical infrastructure and economic resources of the university. The almost self-imposed marginality described by Epeli is as much survival strategy as it is reflection of the status of "culture" in university agendas. One can almost hear the satisfaction in his accounts of the manner in which the *lack* of resources has had the ironic effect of protecting the center from the pressures and politics of external funding.

When I finally had the chance to visit the center a few years ago, I felt that I had wandered into an almost otherworldly place. Walking across the lawn of the quiet USP campus, I was surprised to find the center buzzing with the activity of artists working intently in an amazing variety of media: sculptors working on large wooden pieces outside the building, metal sculptors welding under a canopy, dancers going through their steps on a covered stage, musicians practicing in a recording studio, painters scattered throughout the center surrounded by canvases of work in various phases of completion. Clearly something extraordinary was happening, without so much as a sign to project its presence.

While certainly critical to its success, the physical space of the center is made significant by the work of artists who find their way there to do their work, often inspired by local practices informed by new fusions, media, and performance venues. As Epeli puts it, the center is committed to find inspiration in the "images, sounds, and movements that speak to us, that speak of us in our place and our times." The emphasis on the indigenous and the contemporary described in "Our Place Within" shatters the view that indigenous art is always "traditional" art locked into the past. Unless that confining mindset can be exploded, art knowledge and expertise will always be located elsewhere: in the centers of modernity that value innovation and experimentation over tradition. The genius of the Oceania Centre has been to reinvent assumptions about art, as well as about the indigenous, to allow the production of contemporary work inspired by the experience of living in Oceania. Once accepted, the implications of this view ramify throughout the entire life of the center, calling for the creation of local aesthetics that can be used to evaluate artistic production without always invoking the canons of Western art.

Although the artists do not turn down opportunities to exhibit and sell their work, the center has not actively sought tourist audiences or external marketing. To this day there is no website that describes its programs or features work for sale, whether paintings, sculptures, or CDs. By the same token, focusing on practice and production rather than teaching bears little sign of the gatekeeping practices of academic institutions that might disbar the involvement of local artists. As Epeli has stated, the center is "not a school"; it is "a home for the arts." Prospective artists ask: "How do we enroll?" "How much does it cost?" To which they are told: "Nothing. Just come up." Epeli adds, "For some we give bus fare."

In practice, Epeli's low-key account belies a space of constant activity in the visual arts, performing arts, and music. With modest beginnings the center has gradually established itself as a major presence in the Pacific art scene. In terms of music, for example, it has now produced a list of CDs bringing the work of new artists to regional audiences, often reviving or adapting older styles. Thus a recording of nose flute music released in 2005 was composed and performed by a musician who adapted new styles for an instrument that, formerly widespread, had survived only in Tonga and Hawai'i. The inspiration for this project came from a visiting Native Hawaiian—just as musical ideas might have circulated in the trade networks that Epeli remembers from his New Guinea childhood.

The center's visual artists are also finding wider and wider audiences for their work. In 2004 I had a chance encounter with the Oceania Centre's Red Wave Collective installing an exhibition of recent paintings at the Sheraton Hotel in Nadi, Fiji, where I was waiting for a plane connection. The day before I had rung Epeli in Suva and he informed me that he and some of the artists would be coming the next day to the Sheraton. Appearing with their work in a single van like a band of gypsies, the Oceania Centre's artists completely transformed a routine hanging of pretty landscapes in a hotel gallery into a strong statement about new forms grounded in Oceanian subjects and styles that defy easy categorization.

Oceania Centre painters are redefining the idea of a Pacific art scene—one that is not centered in one of the better-endowed metropoles of Auckland, Sydney, or Noumea. At the same time, center artists and performers find themselves traveling to such venues with increasing frequency, showing or performing their work in festivals and events around the region. In May and June 2006, six artists from the Red Wave Collective showed their work in the October Gallery in the center of London's prestigious art district. Billed as the "first exhibition of its kind in Europe," this exhibit suggests that new Oceanian art will continue to expand its horizons in new directions.

Apart from the growing artistic accomplishments inspired by the center, Epeli sees a broader range of effects both personal and collective. He feels he is "no longer shackled"; he says he is "free to breathe again, to dream the impossible and do something about it." The key in his view is the ability to overcome the psychology of belittlement and the feelings of helplessness it creates. These dreams and visions are more than a kind of self-therapy. They also enable a new politics of engagement with contemporary forces of change. Along with the psychology of belittlement comes vulnerability to pressures that constantly impinge on island societies—such as the new religions that today constitute a "second missionization" repeating much of the colonial past.

It is here that the deployment of the ocean as a metaphor becomes a weapon of and for the weak. Epeli suggests that the ocean offers a trope for perpetual motion and freedom as well as for vastness and depth. In his essay "The Ocean in Us," Epeli articulates the practical value of oceanic metaphors for building the kind of regional identity that has been nurtured over the course of decades at the University of the South Pacific. In his view, a larger regional identity is strategically significant because it enables Oceanians the better to represent their interests in relation to the states and societies of other regions, including Asia, Europe, and North America. Issues as critical as nuclear testing, exploitation of sea resources, and now climate change cannot be taken on by individual communities. They require regional and global solutions. Just as Oceanian ancestors once explored and settled an expanding horizon, so Epeli seeks to articulate an expanded vision of island identity capable of affording a stronger footing in today's engagements with the forces of globalization. At the onset of the Fiji coup in 2000, the USP Laucala Campus was closed down for several months. Students were sent back home to their island countries. The Oceania Centre, however, carried on as usual. As Epeli would say, "You cannot close down an ocean."

One of the many ironies of this collection is that it will appear shortly after two sad events that thrust the author's home, Tonga, into world news. First came the death of the king, eloquently eulogized in the concluding part of this book. That historic event was soon followed by a convulsion of urban violence that saw the destruction of eighty percent of the CBD of the Tongan capital, Nuku'alofa. Both events remind Oceanians that the region is caught up in powerful forces transforming the Pacific with yet unknown effects. They also remind us that, more than ever, meaningful responses to these forces will have to come from Pacific Islanders—from the kind of wisdom evident in Epeli's writing.

Although Epeli's writings promote a recentering of thought and practice in Oceanian experience, his is not an exclusivist agenda. Given that assertions of cultural identity are typically concerned with declaring differences and drawing boundaries, Epeli's Oceania is startlingly expansive and inclusive. Here again, oceans provide metaphors that allow openness and connection. In his words:

> You can claim a piece of land. I have a ten-acre piece of land outside of Suva. You can't do that to the ocean. All we can say is that we belong. The ocean always moves. It's not just us in the middle somewhere there. . . . We are connected to Asia, to the Americas. I hope somehow in the future to make connections with America and places right around the Pacific, to tell our stories and see what we can do together. . . .

This project has been realized through the collaborative effort of numerous people. Robert Kiste gave needed support at the start and a small conspiratorial group including David Hanlon and Houston Wood kept things going. The latter two offered helpful comments on this foreword, as did Barbara Hau'ofa. I am grateful to the participants in the East-West Center's 2003 Summer Institute "Re-Imagining Indigenous Cultures" for discussions referenced here. Unless otherwise noted, quotations derive from that context.

Preface

WHEN CONTACTED about the publication of a collection of my writings, I was concerned because I had written neither sufficiently nor voluminously to merit a respectable tome. I normally write short pieces with the frequency of visits by Halley's Comet. This collection is therefore a miniature tome, rather like an even more stunted bonsai.

The first and last pieces in the collection, "Anthropology and Pacific Islanders" and "Blood in the Kava Bowl," were both written in 1975; the first just before I left the West and the last very soon after my final return to Oceania. Although I no longer write with such heat of passion, the fire is still burning, but now in the early evenings under starlit skies, the best setting for conversation and the telling of stories. Four of the chapters in the volume—"Our Sea of Islands," "The Ocean in Us," "Pasts to Remember," and "Our Place Within"—represent the route that I have travelled in the past fifteen years. It has led me into exciting worlds of ideas, passions, and practice. It has been a journey of joy, discovery, and, I hope, of some service to our widely dispersed communities.

This volume would not have come about without the generous assistance of Geoffrey White, David Hanlon, Houston Wood, and Masako Ikeda. Through Geoffrey, they suggested the idea of it, and helped in putting it all together and shepherding its passage through the publishing process. I wish to express here my profound appreciation of the long, continuous support and encouragement of my work by friends at the Center for Pacific Islands Studies of the University of Hawai'i at Mānoa, the Pacific Islands Development Program of the East-West Center, and in particular my gratitude to the ancient spirits of Hawai'i who always welcome me to their land and shower me with inspiration and aloha.

PART I

Rethinking

OVERLEAF: *Dusia na yalo dina,* Josaia McNamara, 2001

Anthropology and Pacific Islanders

It is a painful experience for people to sit and listen to someone talking about himself. But the theme of this symposium and my rather peculiar situation warrant a personal statement that I shall make as briefly as possible. I speak this morning from two standpoints: firstly, as someone who is undergoing training in a particular academic discipline that binds me intellectually with fellow anthropologists, mostly from the West; and secondly as a native of the South Pacific Islands whose cultures have provided, for nearly a century, a very substantial part of the field of exploitation for our anthropological enterprise. As an aspiring anthropologist, I am intellectually part of an international community bound together by a particular discipline; as a Pacific Islander, I am emotionally tied to peoples in a geographical region, some of whom have achieved independent nationhood, and some who have yet to become autonomous. Whatever their political situation may be, most educated people in the Pacific, like myself, are trying to redefine their cultural identities, or endeavouring to shed a kind of mentality bred under conditions of colonialism. And it is within this context that I shall discuss some aspects of what I consider to be the position of our discipline in the esteem of the peoples of the South Seas.

As a former tutor in the University of Papua New Guinea and someone to whom Islanders talk with little self-conscious politeness or deference, I have been struck by claims that "anthropologists do not really understand us," "do not present a complete or fair picture of us," and, as Tongans say, "do not know how we feel."

Recently, I have been told that in New Guinea, among some sensitive university graduates, we are regarded with distaste. This attitude, of course, is not confined to people in our traditional fieldwork areas; I am certain that many people of the New South Wales town of Bowral feel the same way about Dr. Wilde, as is evident in the views that they expressed in a Four Corners T.V. programme last year. But I am not dealing with what New

South Welshmen think about anthropologists; I am specifically concerned with the reactions of educated Pacific Islanders to us, and their attitudes to the products of our work. Before we dismiss the complaints as the voices of people who are incapable of standing back from their cultural milieu and looking at it with the disinterested objectivity of trained social scientists, we should try first to see what are the grounds, if any, for such complaints. A discussion of these is important in that it may help us in reassessing our relationships with Pacific peoples who are living in a world considerably different from that which Malinowski and his intellectual descendants saw. I exclude from this paper the Maori of New Zealand and the Aborigines of Australia because these groups live in predominantly Western-type societies and their problems are different from those of the largely indigenous populations of the rest of the Pacific isles.

I believe that a major part of the problem is the disjunction between people's expectations of us—probably they would like us to draw portraits of them—and of our special social scientific aims. At times this arises from the fact that when we explain our purposes to those among whom we conduct our fieldwork, we feel unable to explain fully to them our real aims. This is so partly because of the problems of communication that we all know. What we often end up saying is that we are there to learn their customs and to write books about them. They cooperate with us thinking that we are going to tell their stories taking their points of view into consideration. When we produce our articles and monographs and they and their children or grandchildren read them, they often cannot see themselves or they see themselves being distorted and misrepresented. In many cases our field of discourse, and our special social scientific language, preclude any comprehension of what we are talking about even to those who have started training in anthropology. Thus, for example, in the late 1960s perhaps the most popular first-year subject taught at the University of Papua New Guinea was the introductory course in social anthropology. Students flocked to it partly because of the belief that anthropology, which purportedly deals with their traditional cultures and societies, would help them with their problems of alienation and partly to see what we are saying about them. Their interest dropped rapidly once they were confronted with our esoteric language. I do not think that we have produced at the University of Papua New Guinea a native graduate who has entered our profession. As in other parts of the Pacific, students are attracted more to history that deals with their past as people.

Essentially, what Pacific peoples expect of us is to be more of the novelist and the social historian and less of the scientist who speaks in jargon. We do not see ourselves as novelists and rightly so; but we could benefit from the approach of the social historian—and from writing in plain, elegant English. Discussing the attitudes of Africans to Europeans in Ghana before independence, Gustav Jahoda has this to say:

> The skilled writer or novelist sometimes succeeds in conveying to his readers a balanced impression and the "feel" of the strengths and weaknesses, joys and fears, of a whole people. When a psychologist or sociologist digs below the level of overt behaviour, some of the generalisations he comes up with are apt to look odd, distorted, and unflattering. [1961, 132]

I would go a bit further than Jahoda and assert that some of our writings, especially about Melanesians, actually distort the images of those we have studied. Some of the titles of our books, for example *The Sexual Life of Savages,* are very offensive. It needs only one or two instances of gross distortion, especially in books or articles regarded as influential and essential reading, for our discipline to come under wholesale condemnation by the increasingly sensitive educated men and women. Let me offer a good example. Somehow or other we have projected onto Melanesian leaders the caricature of the quintessential Western capitalist: grasping, manipulative, calculating, and without a stitch of morality. Lest it be charged that I am grossly exaggerating, I shall quote an extract from a famous paper on political types in Melanesia and Polynesia:

> Here I find it useful to apply characterisations—or is it caricature?—from our own history to big-men and chiefs. . . . The Melanesian big-man seems so thoroughly bourgeois, so reminiscent of the free enterprising rugged individual of our own heritage. He combines with an ostensible interest in the general welfare a more profound measure of self-interested cunning and economic calculation. His gaze . . . is fixed unswervingly to the main chance. His every public action is designed to make a competitive and invidious comparison with others, to show a standing above the masses that is product of his own personal manufacture. [Sahlins 1963, 164]

The language used here has been taken straight from the factory and the boardroom. The writer denies that traditional Melanesian leaders have any genuine interest in the welfare of their people and insists that their public actions are all motivated purely by selfishness. This is erroneous, and it would have mattered less had it not been for the fact that the article is required reading in Pacific Anthropology. It is an invidious pseudo-evolutionary comparison between the "developed" Polynesian polities and the "underdeveloped" Melanesian ones. It belongs to a genre of literature on Oceania—going back at least two hundred years—written by explorers, navigators, beachcombers, missionaries, colonial officials, and the like who have romanticised Polynesians and denigrated Melanesians. It has been read by hundreds and probably thousands of university students and other interested readers in the English-speaking world and now by students in the Pacific. It has been reprinted in a number of anthropological textbooks. It has the potential of bolstering the long-standing Polynesian racism against Melanesians; and Melanesian students were, in my time, not particularly pleased to read about themselves being unfavourably compared with their eastern neighbours.

This may be an extreme example, but it is indicative of the fact that after decades of anthropological field research in Melanesia we have come up only with pictures of people who fight, compete, trade, pay bride-price, engage in rituals, invent cargo cults, copulate, and sorcerise each other. There is hardly anything in our literature to indicate whether these people have any such sentiments as love, kindness, consideration, altruism, and so on. We cannot tell from our ethnographic writings whether they have a sense of humour. We know little about their systems of morality, specifically their ideas of the good and the bad, and their philosophies; though we sometimes get around to these, wearing dark glasses, through our fascination with cargo cults. We have ignored their physical gestures, their deportment, and their patterns of nonverbal communication. By presenting incomplete and distorted representations of Melanesians we have bastardised our discipline, we have denied people important aspects of their humanity in our literature, and we have thereby unwittingly contributed to the perpetuation of the outrageous stereotypes of them made by ignorant outsiders who lived in their midst.

We should not, therefore, be surprised when we see equally distorted pictures, painted by angry nationalists, depicting them as being more moral and better human beings than us. These are reactions against years of indignities heaped upon them. We talk about this in conversations among ourselves, but we do not care enough to write it down. We are not even aware that in Papua New Guinea we, and through us our discipline, are being increasingly blamed for most of the nasty stereotypes of the people. We are generally innocent of the sins of commission, but we are guilty of the sins of omission and of insensitivity. We tend to be smug and complacent in our self-generated, self-perpetuated, and self-righteous image of ourselves as being better than any other category of foreigners in Melanesia. We congratulate ourselves for being of economic and medical benefit to the communities we study through our free dispensation of medicines, old clothes, some money, and sticks of tobacco to the natives. We assume that because we live for one and a half years or so in their villages and partake of their foods, people must judge us kindly. Today we are judged not so much on that as on our writings. It will not be through our interference in the affairs of Pacific nations that we improve our relationship with Pacific people; rather it will be on the basis of what we have written, what we are writing, and what we will write.

It is fair to say that in general we have contributed insufficiently in our professional writings towards redressing the distorted image of Melanesians. We have neglected to portray them as rounded human beings who love as well as hate, who laugh joyously as well as quarrel, who are peaceful as well as warlike, and who are generous and kindly as well as mean and calculating. Yet it is these ignored qualities that have enabled us to enter unsolicited and live among them. How, then, have we anthropologists neglected these aspects of human existence in Melanesia? Have the models we have taken to the field, for example, that of conflict, blinded us to these qualities? If we are really concerned about our relationships with peoples among whom we have lived—as well as about the future of our discipline in the region—then we have to take into serious consideration the people's increasing sensitivity and touchiness about their image and then infuse into our scientific writings about their cultures and societies some elements of the humanist outlook. I do not advocate compromising our discipline to suit changes in the political winds; what I and many other Pacific men and women would appeal for is balance. When we distort the realities with which we are concerned, we not only offend people who have given us their hospitality and confidence; we also bring into question the validity of our science.

In 1972, Derek Freeman published an article in which he corrected the spelling errors of more than one hundred and seventy Samoan words made by Margaret Mead in her book *Social Organization of Manu'a.* He notes not only Mead's failure to consult Pratt's Samoan dictionary, which sets down the orthography of the language, but also the failure of the Bishop Museum to take heed of his warning about the errors before it issued a new edition of the book. As we are so particular about the spelling of English words I find it deplorable that we do not apply the same standard to our spelling of Pacific languages. Those of us who see and understand the indignation in Freeman's publication are already on the road towards comprehending a little of the reactions of Pacific peoples when important elements of their cultures are abused and their feelings are thoughtlessly or contemptuously disregarded by eminent anthropologists.

A fair indication of the interest in our discipline that we have aroused among the educated people of the region is the fact that, after so many years of involvement, we have produced only one native professional anthropologist, the late Dr. Rusiate Nayacakalou, and that was about fifteen or so years ago. I am a probable poor second. Yet we do not seem to care. We are eager to give all manner of advice to Pacific governments on how to handle their developmental problems; we are willing to give handouts; but we have not discussed as a serious proposition the desirability of the existence of fully qualified native anthropologists to work side by side with their international colleagues on the basis of equality. Since I have been in Australia as a student of anthropology, only one person, Professor Peter Lawrence, has raised the subject with me. So far our concern in this direction has been to involve Pacific peoples in our research projects only in the capacity of field assistants, which is paternalism in the extreme.

While we are steeped in our preoccupation with our own problems of trying to maintain access to our traditional fieldwork areas, we should also give serious thought to encouraging actively the rise of fully trained local colleagues, as far as is possible, in each Pacific country. If we act on this it will be a more lasting and valuable contribution to the region, and to our discipline, than the kinds of tokenism we have so far entertained. There are several good reasons for this.

Firstly, the longer we, as outsiders, monopolise the research in the region, the stronger will be the feelings against us and the more difficult will be our task of extricating our discipline from the taint of imperialism and exploitation.

Secondly, things being equal, local anthropologists, by their very presence in their own societies, should be in an excellent position for conducting continuous research and keeping in touch with local happenings. Those of us who live outside the region have our own commitments to our institutions and societies, and we find it difficult to visit our fieldwork areas as often as we would like. We tend to be absent for many years, and sometimes we do not even return at all. We thus lose the immediacy of the lived-in reality; people and events become blurred images in our memories; so we inevitably write things that come out flat and lifeless, or we escape into ever refined analyses of kinship terminologies that are of no value or interest to humankind except to ourselves.

Thirdly, local anthropologists should have an advantage that most of us lack—namely a thorough knowledge and deep appreciation of the nuances of their own languages. This is one reason why we are often unable to produce multidimensional representations of the realities we deal with: although we may be proficient in the languages of those among whom we conduct our fieldwork, we generally do not have the appreciation that local speakers do. The time we spend in the field is too short. I speak here in terms of averages; there are notable exceptions.

Finally, local anthropologists should have the intuitive knowledge and a built-in "feel" for the subtleties of their cultures and their human relationships. Cynics and people without vision say that natives are too stupid or too closely involved in their own societies to be objective in their research. Let us face facts: everywhere men and women of ability and wisdom can and do overcome great difficulties. Professor Meyer Fortes (pers. comm.) has pointed out that West African anthropologists—who, significantly, call themselves sociologists—are not different from their British and other non-African colleagues in terms of their products. Despite their initial advantages, he adds, African social scientists have not produced anything that others have not been able to accomplish. This is so because African anthropologists were trained in the rigours of uncompromising empiricism and other Western intellectual traditions that had effectively suppressed any expression of the subjective insights they might have into their own communities. We must devise ways—or, better still, widen the horizon of our discipline—in order to tap instead of suppress the subjectivity to which I have referred and thereby humanise our study of the conditions of the peoples and cultures of the Pacific.

Note

This essay is a revised form of a paper I read to the symposium "The Future of Anthropology in Melanesia" at the 46th ANZAAS Congress held in Canberra in January 1975. The paper was subsequently published in *Oceania* 45 (1975):283–

289. From the original paper I have deleted some words and added roughly one typed page. I wish to express my appreciation to Marie Reay, who was immensely helpful in discussing some of the ideas expressed in the essay; Inge Riebe, who read an early draft and pronounced it too tame; and Barbara Hau'ofa, who reads my mind and says wise and critical things that are not always flattering.

References

Freeman, D. 1972. "Social Organization of Manu'a (1930 and 1969). By Margaret Mead: Some Errata." *Journal of the Polynesian Society* 81:1.

Jahoda, G. 1961. *White Man.* London: Oxford University Press.

Sahlins, M. G. 1963. "Poor Man, Rich Man, Big Man, Chief: Political Types in Melanesia and Polynesia." Reprinted in *Readings in Australian and Pacific Anthropology,* edited by I. Hogbin and L. R. Hiatt. Melbourne: Melbourne University Press, 1966.

The New South Pacific Society

Integration and Independence

I WOULD LIKE to advance the view that there already exists in our part of the world a single regional economy upon which has emerged a South Pacific society, the privileged groups of which share a single dominant culture with increasingly marginalised local subcultures shared by the poorer classes. The regional society is emerging from the process of decolonisation that, contrary to stated intentions, has integrated the Pacific Islands into the Australian/New Zealand economy and society to the extent that the islands cannot or will not disentangle themselves. In view of this integration, we must reexamine many of the assumptions we have about development in our region.

All the countries in the South Pacific have been drawn into a single economic system controlled by transnational industrial, commercial, and financial interests backed and defended by powerful governmental and military organisations working closely with each other. In saying this I do not propose to enter into a discussion of the world economy; I confine myself to our South Pacific region because it directly and immediately concerns us. By isolating our region from the world economy I do not imply that ours is in any way a closed system; rather our region is a distinct subgroup of the global unit, a subgrouping based on geographic alignment and on a growing multiplicity of economic, social, and cultural ties including a common concern with the security and well-being of our part of the world. By "South Pacific" I mean the region covered by Australia and Papua New Guinea in the west, Kiribati in the north, New Zealand in the south, and the Cook Islands in the east. I would also include French Polynesia and New Caledonia, whose full membership in our regional subgrouping is but a matter of time.

It is probably true to say that no major geographic region in the world is as integrated as the South Pacific. We are, for all practical purposes, a single economy and increasingly a single society. All the economies of the

South Pacific Forum countries are so tied to that of Australia and New Zealand that they cannot be considered separate entities. In addition to trade and industries, the financial, transport, and communications systems are tied to New Zealand and Australia. Australia and New Zealand are the major exporters of goods and services to the islands, and in view of the rising costs of transportation, they will maintain this position for some time to come. Australian and New Zealand banks and insurance firms are the major nonnational financial institutions in the islands. The travel industry, which has become a major foreign exchange earner in several island countries, relies heavily on the Australian and New Zealand market and indeed is controlled by their airlines and travel agencies. Qantas and Ansett manage the national airlines of the islands, and together with Air New Zealand they are the major carriers on the regional air routes. The regional shipping service, the Forum Line, which connects the various islands to Australia and New Zealand, depends for its survival upon subsidies from these countries. The prospective development of television broadcasting in the islands seems now to be in the hands of the Sydney-based Channel 9. Radio Australia is the islands' source of information on contemporary world events, and the major daily newspapers are owned by Australian interests. The island regional institutions—such as the South Pacific Commission, the South Pacific Bureau for Economic Cooperation, the University of the South Pacific, the Forum Fisheries, and so forth—rely very much on Australia and New Zealand for funding and staff. And all kinds of development activities in the islands depend to a large extent on Australian and New Zealand aid.

When people view things from the vantage point of national economies, they may be excused for thinking that Australia and New Zealand are the main beneficiaries in the intraregional economic relationships. But when reality is perceived from the point of view of a regional economy, then the answer to the question of who benefits most comes out differently. The main beneficiaries from this point of view are the privileged, elite groups all over the region, not just Australia or New Zealand—groups that are directly or indirectly concerned with economic activities in the South Pacific. These include elements of both the public and private sectors in the islands as well as in Australia and New Zealand. These elite groups are locked to each other through their privileged access to and control of resources moving within the region and between the South Pacific and other regions of the world. They form the ruling tiers of the emerging regional society. I use the word "society" deliberately. Through governmental, business, professional, educational, and other connections, including migration and marriage, members of these groups have forged intimate links to the extent that they have a great deal more in common with each other than with members of the other classes in their own communities. These groups, to which most of us attending this conference belong, form the backbone of the emerging South Pacific society. I include the intelligentsia in these groups because they are the intellectual arm of the ruling classes.

As part of the process of integration and the emergence of the new society, the ruling classes of the South Pacific are increasingly culturally homogeneous: they speak the same language, which is English (this language is becoming the first tongue of an increasing number of children in the islands); they share the same ideologies and the same material lifestyles (admittedly with local variations due to physical environment and original cultural factors, but the similarities are much more numerous than the differences). The privileged classes share a single dominant regional culture; the underprivileged maintain subcultures related to the dominant one through ties of patronage and growing inequality. These localised subcultures are modified versions of indigenous cultures that existed before the capitalist penetration of the South Pacific. Scholars and politicians often point to the enormous diversity and persistence of traditional cultures in the South Pacific as a factor for disunity and economic backwardness at the national and regional levels. But they overlook the fact that today the important differences and problems in development are due not so much to the multiplicity and persistence of indigenous cultures as, increasingly, to the emergence of classes in the region. I suggest that we should not be misled by the existence of subsistence, nonmonetised sectors of economy and by cultural diversity as well as national politics into concluding that there is neither regional integration nor a regional class system. The nonmonetised sectors are being marginalised especially through aided development with its overemphasis on commercial and export-oriented production. Subsistence activities are rapidly becoming the preserve of the poor. Cultural diversity is also largely found among the underprivileged classes especially in rural areas.

Among the privileged there is homogeneity throughout the region through the sharing of a single dominant culture. Variations among these homogeneous groups are minor in character: the differences largely add spice to social intercourse as Chinese, Indian, Lebanese, and other exotic dishes make bourgeois dinner parties more interesting. It is one of the privileges of the affluent classes to have access to a wide range of superficial cultural experiences and expertise; it is the privileged who can afford to tell the poor to preserve their traditions. But their perceptions of which traits of traditional culture to preserve are increasingly divergent from those of the poor. In the final analysis it is the poor who have to live out the traditional culture; the privileged can merely talk about it, and they are in a position to be selective about what traits they use or more correctly urge others to observe; and this is increasingly seen by the poor as part of the ploy by the privileged to secure greater advantages for themselves. I return to this theme later. The point I wish to emphasise now is that the poor in the islands are not so different in their relative deprivation from the poor in New Zealand and Australia. And from the perspective of the regional economy, they all belong to the same underprivileged groups since their deprivation is directly related to the same regional and indeed international development forces and trends that always seem to favour the already privileged.

The Pacific Islands educational systems are an essential tool for promoting greater incorporation into the regional economy and society. They are also a vital instrument for the development of elite groups tied to Australia and New Zealand and increasingly to each other. The medium of instruction in all secondary schools, with the exception of schools in the French colonies, is English. Furthermore, Western Samoa, Fiji, Tonga, Niue, and the Cook Islands follow the New Zealand secondary school system, and their senior students sit for the New Zealand University Entrance examination. Tens of thousands of Polynesian and Fiji Indian minds have been conditioned by the New Zealand educational system as many people of my generation were conditioned by the British system and the Senior Cambridge examination. The difference was that Britain was halfway around the world whereas Australia and New Zealand loom over the horizon in an ineradicable presence. Thousands of Pacific Islanders have attended secondary and tertiary educational institutions in Australia and New Zealand. Thousands of island civil servants have been trained in the Australian School for Pacific Administration at Mossman in Sydney. Given the absolute size of island populations, the proportion of island people affected by the educational systems of Australia and New Zealand, and therefore mentally and emotionally attuned to these countries, is quite staggering. Since these are the people who comprise the ruling classes of their communities, it is not at all surprising that development policies of the islands are increasingly and smoothly synchronised with policies set in Canberra and Wellington, the main centres of control for our region.

In recent years there has been a mounting concern with the relevance of the academic and urban orientation of general education in island communities. Despite this concern nothing really substantial has been done to revise educational curricula apart from adding greater local content to the existing forms. What seems not to have been fully grasped is that the present orientation and policy are the most appropriate to the overall development towards greater regional integration. The idea of tailoring educational systems away from the present preoccupation with academic and urban orientation arises from the basic misconception of islands being territorially bounded economies and societies. Alternatives to the present forms of education can only be effected if the economy is radically altered, which is highly unlikely, or if a dual education system is introduced—that is, the present emphasis will be reserved for the privileged while more rural and technically oriented curricula are devised for the poor. Neither alternative is politically acceptable, at least publicly, although a form of dual system is emerging in Papua New Guinea and Fiji, the two most economically advanced communities in the islands. There are already exclusive "international" schools in these communities, schools that are oriented towards giving children of the ruling classes advantages in training for lucrative positions in the regional economy. The same is true of island universities; the University of the South Pacific, for example, is probably the leading manpower factory in the islands. It aims to fulfil certain training needs of the countries it serves. These needs are defined for the university by island governments and private organisations—the very institutions that are spearheading the integrative development. As such, the university is an arm of the ruling classes in the region; under present circumstances it cannot be anything else.

The overall process of integration has gone much further in Polynesia than in Melanesia and Kiribati. This has been a function of migration from Polynesia to New Zealand and Australia and, as well, the greater reliance of Polynesia on aid. The Cook Islands, Niue, and Tokelau are the most integrated with much more than half of their populations living in New Zealand. Western Samoans, Tongans, and Fiji Indians are not very far behind. Fijians do not emigrate as much as other Polynesians, but as they face greater economic hardship than they face today, more of them will undoubtedly emigrate. The significance of this population mobility is the extension of numerous kinship and other social networks from the islands to New Zealand and Australia, which facilitates a continuous flow of people and resources within the region. For many islanders these networks provide the main source of economic benefits for the poor. But they also contribute greatly to regional integration.

There live in Australia the descendants of the nineteenth-century Melanesian indentured labourers. It is not inconceivable that more of these may attempt to rediscover their roots in Melanesia as black Americans have searched for theirs in Africa. This seems more likely now that Melanesians in their homelands are asserting their cultural identities and are on the verge of forming a Melanesian Alliance. We must also keep in mind the facts that Australia's northern boundary is within a stone's throw of mainland Papua New Guinea and, moreover, that within its borders Australia contains the Torres Strait Islands whose largely Melanesian population has close ethnic affinity with the people of the southwestern coast of Papua New Guinea. A similar situation obtains on the boundary between Papua New Guinea and Solomon Islands. Whether or not population movement between Melanesia and Australia will develop beyond the predominantly circular mobility of today remains to be seen. But it is not beyond the realm of possibility given the regional alignment, the vast natural resources of Melanesia (especially of Papua New Guinea and New Caledonia), and the volatile frontier relationship between Papua New Guinea and Indonesia.

Population movement in the region is not only between the islands and Australia and New Zealand. Each community in the South Pacific contains people from other island groups. Fiji is probably the best example of this. The population of Suva includes people from just about every South Pacific community, and there are islands in Fiji that have been used to resettle excess population from Kiribati and Tuvalu. Because of our preoccupation with the migration of Pacific Islanders to Australia and New Zealand we tend to overlook the glaring and important fact that there are thousands of Australians and New Zealanders living in the islands as migrants—or diplomats, advisers, professionals, businessmen, hired hands of various kinds, even drugrunners and other unsavoury elements. The presence of Australians and New Zealanders in the islands contributes greatly to integration since they tend to occupy powerful or influential positions in both the public and the private sectors. The placement of kinsmen and kinswomen in the various communities in the region adds flesh and blood to the framework of integration.

We should also be mindful of the fact that every year tens of thousands of Australians and New Zealanders travel to the islands as short-term visitors staying in hotels, motels, and guesthouses. Moreover, thousands of Pacific Islanders travel each year to Australia and New Zealand as short-term visitors staying mostly with their relatives. The flow of island visitors to Australia and New Zealand has been largely overlooked by those who study tourism. But anyone who looks into this movement is likely to discover a very important variation of international travel. The short-term circular mobility of ordinary people contributes to awareness of and familiarity with each other, and therefore to the course of regional integration.

In addition, the privileged groups in the islands have forged increasing links with each other, facilitated by such regional institutions as the South Pacific Bureau for Economic Cooperation, the University of the South Pacific, and a host of international organisations such as the agencies of the United Nations. Frequent meetings of representatives of government, business, and educational and other organisations, in the islands as well as in Australia and New Zealand, have contributed to the emergence of an elitist regional identity generally known as the Pacific Way.

One important development is that highly trained Pacific Islanders have become specialists in their various fields and an increasing number of them are entering the arena of consultancy within the region, doing the kinds of lucrative assignments previously the preserve of consultants and advisers from the West. This particular development is very significant. By combining their specialist expertise with their insiders' insights into the workings of island societies, island consultants are becoming more effective for the cause of capitalist development than their non-Islander counterparts. The co-option of island intellectuals into the system is politically judicious; it gives the appearance of localisation and a fair division of labour, not to mention lucre, while at the same time promoting development towards ever greater regionalism.

For many years now it has been recognised that there are common problems—such as the nuclearisation of the Pacific, the impact of superpower rivalry, the exploration and exploitation of resources within the exclusive economic zones, the protection of exclusive economic zone rights, and the stability and security of the South Pacific—that could only be dealt with on a regional basis. Cooperation on these matters further promotes regional integration.

Given the situation that I have just outlined, I suggest that we should reexamine our assumptions about relationships within the South Pacific. The degree to which integration has been achieved has not been acknowledged by the component communities of the region—partly because of particular national interests protecting their own turf and partly because of the hangover from colonialism when Australia and New Zealand were metropolitan powers. Underlying the concern by Australia and New Zealand for the development of the islands are strategic considerations for their own security. The ruling classes of all the communities have now seen the problem of regional security as probably the most important thing they have in common. Australia and New Zealand still see most if not all development in the Pacific in terms of its contribution to their security. For internal political reasons neither country really wants to recognise the extent of economic and social integration that is taking place—an integration that has been a direct outcome of Australia's and New Zealand's concern with their own security, initially as distant and vulnerable outposts of the British Empire and now as affluent communities in a rising sea of poverty. To both these countries the Pacific Islands are of little economic significance; this has been stated publicly by high government officials and by influential academics of both countries.

The Pacific Islands, believing in their alleged economic insignificance, tend to play to the full their strategic value to get as much advantage as they can from Australia and New Zealand. The latest incident of this kind was reported by the *New Zealand Times* of 11 August 1985 in an article with a revealing heading: "Fiji Twists Arms at Forum." It appears that before the Forum meeting in Rarotonga, Prime Minister Bob Hawke received a letter from the prime minister of Fiji. According to the *Times* an extract of Ratu Sir Kamisese Mara's letter reads as follows:

> We have all expressed concern about the ongoing fisheries access negotiations between Kiribati and the Soviet Union. Other countries in the region, including Fiji, have received similar overtures from the Soviet Union. These developments, in my view, make it all the more urgent that Australia and other long-standing friends in the Pacific come forward with further positive, visible and affirmative action in providing supportive economic measures.

> I believe that no island country would feel compelled to enter into new alignments if such support were readily available from within our region.

According to the *Times* Mr. Hawke was so concerned with Mara's letter that while in Fiji on his way to Rarotonga he telephoned New Zealand's prime minister, David Lange, who was then in Western Samoa and also on his way to Rarotonga, seven times in one night to discuss the matter. This arm-twisting game I believe was inaugurated in the early 1970s by the king of Tonga when he announced a forthcoming "affirmative action" deal with the Soviet Union; since then other Pacific countries have joined the game, some using as aces up their sleeves the dreaded names of Cuba and Libya, resulting in "affirmative actions" and "supportive economic measures" from Australia and New Zealand rocketing into orbit—where they have since remained. This regional gamesmanship is reminiscent of the typical torrid, nocturnal negotiations conducted between debauched customers and depraved streetwalkers. This is the kind of situation we find ourselves in when we ignore reality and see our common interests mainly in terms of strategic considerations. If we acknowledge our economic and social integration we will be able to deal with the problem of the security of the South Pacific as an aspect of that integration. This could make a lot of difference in the conduct of our regional relationships.

As pointed out earlier, there is a belief that the Pacific Islands are of little or no economic interest to Australia and New Zealand and, moreover, that these two countries' main concern is to help the islands through aid to achieve increasing self-reliance as part of the decolonisation process. Australia and New Zealand tend to consider the islands as bounded economies and states; the smallest island communities are taken as examples of economic insignificance and burden on their taxpayers. But if we take the region as a whole, the resources of the islands are not so negligible. The mineral resources of Melanesia, especially those of Papua New Guinea and New Caledonia, are of great regional significance. The potential offshore resources within the exclusive economic zones of the region may not be negligible. It may be noted here that the combined exclusive economic zones of all the South Pacific countries cover a very large portion of the earth's surface. When Papua New Guinea was still a colony and a resource-poor country, it was always considered together with the rest of the Pacific Islands. Now that its vast mineral resources have been discovered, Papua New Guinea has been taken off the list of Pacific Islands by Australia and given a special status of its own. This divisive tactic helps to keep alive the image of the Pacific Islands as being of little economic significance.

New Zealand may claim that its aid to a particular small country is far in excess of any economic benefit it gains in return. But New Zealand's overall trade with Pacific Islands as a whole is so much in its favour that its total aid outlay goes only a modest way towards correcting the imbalance. The same is true of Australia—except that much of its monetary aid never leaves the country or it may leave like a tourist only to fly back home in great comfort and loaded with duty-free goods. The point is that when the flows of resources within the region are added up, Australia and New Zealand still come out well ahead. For what they give out in aid they receive in return a great deal more in the forms of export earnings and repatriation of profits on investments. It may be said that as far as the regional relationships are concerned, if the words "aid" and "help" are to be used at all, they should more correctly be used in terms of the small islands "aiding" their two big neighbours.

Another problem with the use of the term "aid" in our region is that it purportedly aims to help the Pacific Islands to become self-reliant so that there will be no need for further aid. But as I have tried to show, instead of increasing self-reliance the development trends over the past decades have been towards economic and social integration. That the Pacific Islands will ever again be truly self-reliant is an impossibility. It is an impossibility not because, as experts say, they lack the necessary resources to be self-reliant—for given a different economy and society they could very well be self-sufficient as they were for centuries until about a hundred years ago. They cannot be self-reliant because they are in an economy that will not allow them to be; they are too much part of the overall regional strategic alignment for the protection of that economy to be allowed any real measure of independence. Furthermore, the ruling classes in the whole region benefit so much from the present arrangements that, despite rhetoric to the contrary, they would have it no other way. What is termed "aid" has in fact turned out to be a necessary corrective and integrative mechanism, and as such will continue unabated and grow, for it does not really cost much to keep a few tiny communities with very small populations within the system. In fact, as I have pointed out, it costs Australia and New Zealand hardly anything to maintain and even to intensify the integration. I have argued elsewhere that there is no such thing as aid.[1] I will not repeat that argument here except to reinforce it by saying that since aid has achieved the complete opposite of its stated aims, it is no longer aid. Either we should adopt a new term for the resource distribution it represents, or we should give it a new and more honest definition.

Development towards self-reliance and full national sovereignty has been the stated goal of decolonisation. But we have seen that decolonisation has led to integration. Without self-reliance there can be no real national sovereignty in the South Pacific islands. It follows that what we call national sovereignty in the region is little more than a measure of local autonomy in the hands of competing national interests within the larger regional economy. These interests are represented by the ruling groups within each community. Their control of the resources within their communities and their privileged access to resources moving through the region make them indispensable to the regional centres located in Australia and New Zealand. Many of the resources including aid moving from these centres to the regional communities go towards the support of elite groups that, as we have seen, have strong economic, social, and cultural ties with Australia and New Zealand. The economic and strategic integration that I have discussed rests on the maintenance of the local ruling classes and their continued affiliation with regional centres of control.

Finally, I think that a very important development, one that we have to watch carefully, is the emergence of privileged classes in the islands. For it is certain that the fates of the island communities are being decided by the ways in which these groups act, first, in relation to their own underprivileged people and, second, in relation to their important connections with each other and with similar groups elsewhere. It has been said that a main problem with Pacific Islanders is their high level of material aspirations—that they desire goods and services which their own communities' resources cannot provide. An immediate reaction to this is to say that this is so because Pacific Islanders are part of an economy that thrives on consumerism. To have drawn people into an economy dominated by Australia and New Zealand and then to expect them to have aspirations different from Australians and New Zealanders is to expect something that is not in the nature of human beings. A further examination of the problem would reveal that people's aspirations are not uniformly high. We would most likely see that the levels of aspiration vary according to social classes. The highest levels would be found among the privileged; the poor merely struggle to survive and scrounge for what they can get from the effluent of the affluent. The privileged have high aspirations because they can generally get what they want through their ability to plug into the wider economy and, as well, by strictly regulating the access to the same resources by others. The underprivileged are poor because of their inability to tap the regional resources and are therefore left to make the best out of what is available in their immediate physical surroundings.

There are people who believe that our economy is wrong and that the conditions of the underprivileged in the islands will continue to deteriorate. My experiences over the last decade have led me towards the same conclusion. But I also think that, in the short-term future at least, the present system will continue and that in the South Pacific there cannot be any real change without fundamental structural alterations in Islander relations with Australia and New Zealand, the twin hubs of our region. It is no longer realistic to say that each island country must be able to clean up its own house. Those who wish to see Pacific Islanders living at the levels their own national resources can support overlook the obvious fact that there are no bounded economies in the region. Given that situation, the problem of the poor remains—or perhaps I should say that the problem of the affluent remains. It is the privileged who decide on the needs of their communities and the directions of development and whose rising aspirations and affluence entail the worsening conditions of the poor. I deliberately state this truism because it is something relatively new to the islands. There is a strong reluctance on the part of the regional privileged, including academics, to recognise the emergence of modern classes in the island world. There is a tendency for island analysts, businessmen, state officials, and politicians, influenced by their Western mentors, to blame the poor for their own conditions. They are said to be too culture-bound to see things as they should be seen and act accordingly. If they could only be less traditional and less indolent, pull up their socks (as if they had any to begin with), and adopt the Protestant Work Ethic, they could easily raise their standards of living. I submit that this is a red herring. Firstly, the problem is not so much a cultural issue of stubborn adherence to outmoded traditions as it is an economic matter. The poor adhere to some of their traditions because they have consistently been denied any real benefits from their labour. Their adherence to their traditions is a matter of necessity and economic security. Given real opportunities within the larger economy, they would more than pull up their socks: witness the rush of Polynesians to the factories of New Zealand, Australia, and the United States when real opportunities and alternatives were in the offing.

Secondly, the very sections in island communities that preach against adherence to "outmoded traditions" are the very groups that simultaneously try to force the dead weight of other traditions on the poor. This is especially true of parts of Polynesia where aristocratic rules and Christian church traditions, combined with the depredations of the emerging bourgeoisie, have inflicted suffering on the poor. Increasingly the privileged and the poor observe different traditions, each adhering to those that serve their interest best. The difference is that the poor merely live by their preferred traditions while the privileged often try to force certain other traditions on the poor in order to maintain social stability—that is, in order to secure the privileges that they have gained, not so much from their involvement in traditional activities as from their privileged access to resources in the regional economy. In such a situation, traditions are used by the ruling classes to enforce the new order.

Notes

This essay is a revised version of a speech delivered at the Conference on Pacific Studies, University of Auckland, August 1985. It was published in *Class and Culture in the South Pacific,* edited by Antony Hooper et al. (Auckland: Centre for Pacific Studies, University of Auckland; Suva: Institute of Pacific Studies, University of the South Pacific, 1987).

1. I am referring here to another paper that I delivered in Australia.

PART II

Reflecting

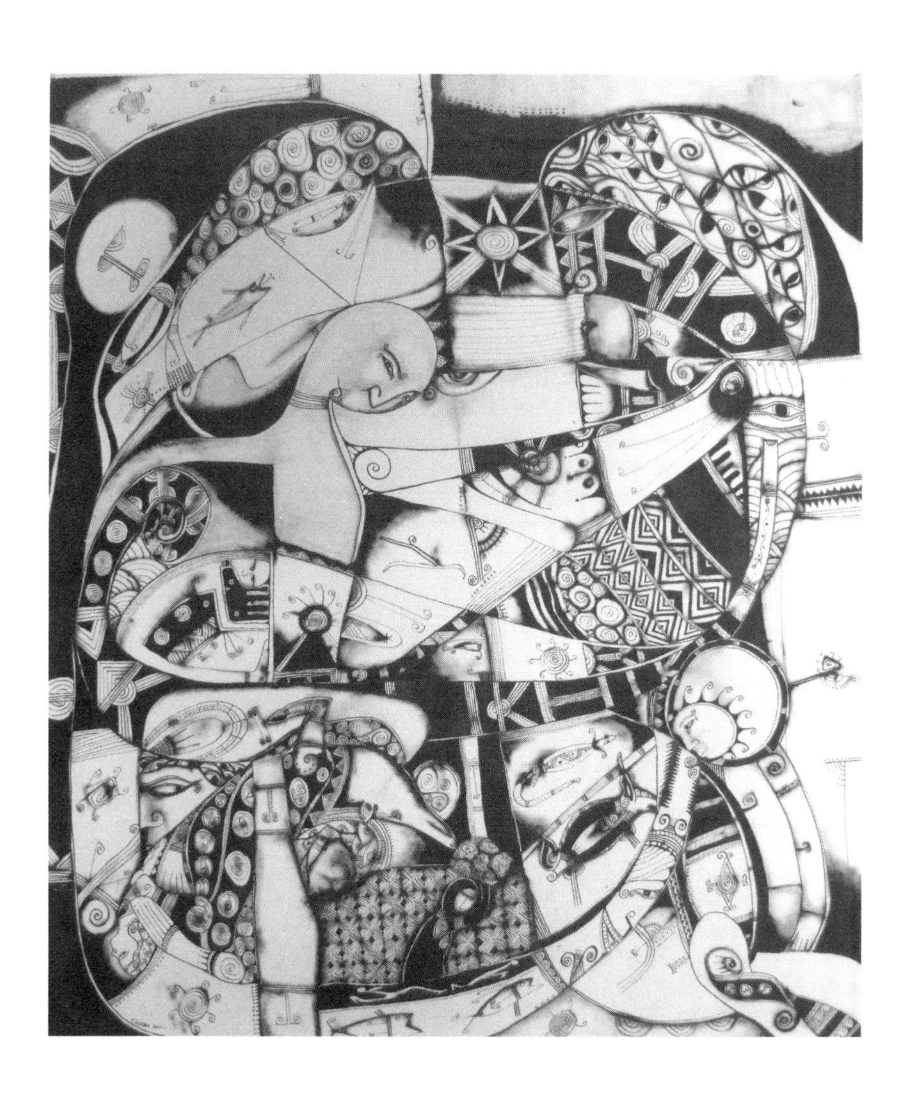

OVERLEAF: *The Voyage,* Frederick Butafa, 2001

Our Sea of Islands

THIS ESSAY raises some issues of great importance to our region and offers a view of Oceania that is new and optimistic. What I say here is likely to disturb a number of men and women who have dedicated their lives to Oceania and for whom I hold the greatest respect and affection and always will.

In our region, two levels of operation are pertinent to the purposes of this essay. The first level is that of national governments and regional and international diplomacy, in which the present and future of Pacific Island states and territories are planned and decided on. Discussions here are the preserve of politicians, bureaucrats, statutory officials, diplomats, the military, and representatives of the financial and business communities, often in conjunction with donor and international lending organisations, and advised by academic and consultancy experts. Much that passes at this level concerns aid, concessions, trade, investment, defence, and security, matters that have taken the Pacific further and further into dependency on powerful nations.

The other level is that of ordinary people, peasants and proletarians, who, because of the poor flow of benefits from the top, scepticism about stated policies and the like, tend to plan and make decisions about their lives independently, sometimes with surprising and dramatic results that go unnoticed or ignored at the top. Moreover, academic and consultancy experts tend to overlook or misinterpret grassroots activities because they do not fit with prevailing views about the nature of society and its development.

Views of the Pacific from the level of macroeconomics and macropolitics often differ markedly from those at the level of ordinary people. The vision of Oceania presented here is based on my observations of behaviour at the grass roots.

Having clarified my vantage point, let me make a statement of the obvious: views held by those in dominant positions about their subordinates can have significant consequences for people's self-image and for the ways they cope with their situations. Such views, often derogatory and belittling, are integral to most relationships of dominance and subordination, wherein superiors behave in ways or say things that are accepted by their inferiors, who in turn behave in ways that perpetuate the relationships.

In Oceania, derogatory and belittling views of indigenous cultures are traceable to the early years of interaction with Europeans. The wholesale condemnation by Christian missionaries of Oceanian cultures as savage, lascivious, and barbaric has had a lasting and negative effect on people's views of their histories and traditions. In a number of Pacific societies people still divide their history into two parts: the era of darkness, associated with savagery and barbarism, and the era of light and civilisation ushered in by Christianity.

In Papua New Guinea, European males were addressed as "masters" and workers as "boys." Even indigenous policemen were called "police boys." This use of language helped to reinforce the colonially established social stratification along ethnic divisions. Colonial practices and denigration portrayed Melanesian peoples and cultures as even more primitive and barbaric than those of Polynesia. In this light, Melanesian attempts during the immediate postcolonial years to rehabilitate their cultural identity by cleansing it of its colonial taint are natural reactions. Leaders like Walter Lini of Vanuatu and Bernard Narokobi of Papua New Guinea have spent much of their energy extolling the virtues of Melanesian values as equal to if not better than those of their erstwhile colonisers.

Europeans did not invent belittlement. In many societies it was part and parcel of indigenous cultures. In the aristocratic societies of Polynesia, parallel relationships of dominance and subordination with their paraphernalia of appropriate attitudes and behaviour were the order of the day. In Tonga, the term for commoners is *me'a vale,* "the ignorant ones," which is a survival from an era when the aristocracy controlled all important knowledge in the society. Keeping the ordinary folk in the dark and calling them ignorant made it easier to control and subordinate them.

I would like, however, to focus on a currently prevailing notion about Islanders and their physical surroundings that, if not countered with more constructive views, could inflict lasting damage on people's images of themselves and on their ability to act with relative autonomy in their endeavours to survive reasonably well within the international system in which they have found themselves. It is a belittling view that has been propagated unwittingly—mostly by social scientists who have sincere concern for the welfare of Pacific peoples. According to this view, the small island states and territories of the Pacific, that is, all of Polynesia and Micronesia, are too small, too poorly endowed with resources, and too isolated from the centres of economic growth for their inhabitants ever to be able to rise above their present condition of dependence on the largesse of wealthy nations.

Initially I not only agreed wholeheartedly with this perspective but participated actively in its propagation. It seemed to be based on irrefutable evidence—on the reality of our existence. Events of the 1970s and 1980s confirmed the correctness of this view. The hoped-for era of autonomy following political independence did not materialise. Our national leaders were in the vanguard of a rush to secure financial aid from every quarter; our economies were stagnating or declining; our environments were deteriorating or threatened and we could do little about it; our own people were evacuating themselves to greener pastures elsewhere. Whatever remained of our resources, including our exclusive economic zones, was being hawked for the highest bid. Some of our islands had become, in the words of one social scientist, "MIRAB societies"—pitiful microstates condemned forever to depend on migration, remittances, aid, and bureaucracy, not on any real economic productivity. Even the better-resource-endowed Melanesian countries were mired in dependency, indebtedness, and seemingly endless social fragmentation and political instability. What hope was there for us?

This bleak view of our existence was so relentlessly pushed that I began to be concerned about its implications. I tried to find a way out but could not. Then two years ago I began noticing the reactions of my students when I explained our situation of dependence. Their faces crumbled visibly, they asked for solutions, I could offer none. I was so bound to the notion of smallness that even if we improved our approaches to production, for example, the absolute size of our islands would still impose such severe limitations that we would be defeated in the end.

But the faces of my students continued to haunt me mercilessly. I began asking questions of myself. What kind of teaching is it to stand in front of young people from your own region, people you claim as your own, who have come to university with high hopes for the future, and you tell them that our countries are hopeless? Is this not what neocolonialism is all about? To make people believe that they have no choice but to depend?

Soon the realisation dawned on me. In propagating a view of hopelessness, I was actively participating in our own belittlement. I then decided to do something about it. But I thought that since any new perspective must confront some of the sharpest and most respected minds in the region, it must be well researched and thought out if it was to be taken seriously. It was a daunting task, and I hesitated.

Then came invitations for me to speak at Kona and Hilo on the Big Island of Hawai'i at the end of March 1993. The lecture at Kona, to a meeting of the Association of Social Anthropologists in Oceania, was written before I left Suva. The speech at the University of Hawai'i at Hilo was forming in my mind and was to be written when I got to Hawai'i. I had decided to try out my new perspective even though it had not been properly researched. I could hold back no longer. The drive from Kona to Hilo was my "road to Damascus." I saw such scenes of grandeur as I had not seen before: the eerie blackness of regions covered by recent volcanic eruptions; the remote majesty of Mauna Loa, long and smooth, the world's largest volcano; the awesome craters of Kīlauea threatening to erupt at any moment; and the lava flow on the coast not far away. Under the aegis of Pele, before my very eyes, the Big Island was growing, rising from the depths of a mighty sea. The world of Oceania is not small; it is huge and growing bigger every day.

The idea that the countries of Polynesia and Micronesia are too small,[1] too poor, and too isolated to develop any meaningful degree of autonomy is an economistic and geographic deterministic view of a very narrow kind that overlooks culture history and the contemporary process of what may be called world enlargement that is carried out by tens of thousands of ordinary Pacific Islanders right across the ocean—from east to west and north to south, under the very noses of academic and consultancy experts, regional and international development agencies, bureaucratic planners and their advisers, and customs and immigration officials—making nonsense of all national and economic boundaries, borders that have been defined only recently, crisscrossing an ocean that had been boundless for ages before Captain Cook's apotheosis.

If this very narrow, deterministic perspective is not questioned and checked, it could contribute importantly to an eventual consignment of whole groups of human beings to a perpetual state of wardship wherein they and their surrounding lands and seas would be at the mercy of the manipulators of the global economy and "world orders" of one kind or another. Belittlement in whatever guise, if internalised for long and transmitted across generations, may lead to moral paralysis, to apathy, to the kind of fatalism we can see among our fellow human beings who have been herded and confined to reservations or internment camps. People in some of our islands are in danger of being confined to mental reservations if not physical ones. I am thinking here of people in the Marshall Islands, who have been victims of atomic and missile tests by the United States.

Do people in most of Oceania live in tiny confined spaces? The answer is yes if one believes what certain social scientists are saying. But the idea of smallness is relative; it depends on what is included and excluded in any calculation of size. When those who hail from continents or from islands adjacent to continents—and the vast majority of human beings live in these regions—when they see a Polynesian or Micronesian island they naturally pronounce it small or tiny. Their calculation is based entirely on the extent of the land surfaces they see.

But if we look at the myths, legends, and oral traditions, indeed the cosmologies of the peoples of Oceania, it becomes evident that they did not conceive of their world in such microscopic proportions. Their universe comprised not only land surfaces but the surrounding ocean as far as they could traverse and exploit it, the underworld with its fire-controlling and earth-shaking denizens, and the heavens above with their hierarchies of powerful gods and named stars and constellations that people could count on to guide their ways across the seas. Their world was anything but tiny. They thought big and recounted their deeds in epic proportions. One legendary Oceanian athlete was so powerful that during a competition he threw his javelin with such force that it pierced the horizon and disappeared until that night when it was seen streaking across the sky like a meteor. Every now and then it reappears to remind people of the mighty deed. And as far as I'm concerned it is still out there, near Jupiter or somewhere. That was the first rocket ever sent into space. Islanders today still relish exaggerating things out of all proportion. Smallness is a state of mind.

There is a world of difference between viewing the Pacific as "islands in a far sea" and as "a sea of islands."[2] The first emphasises dry surfaces in a vast ocean far from the centres of power. Focussing in this way stresses the smallness and remoteness of the islands. The second is a more holistic perspective in which things are seen in the totality of their relationships.

I return to this point later. Continental men, namely Europeans, on entering the Pacific after crossing huge expanses of ocean, introduced the view of "islands in a far sea." From this perspective the islands are tiny, isolated dots in a vast ocean. Later on, continental men—Europeans and Americans—drew imaginary lines across the sea, making the colonial boundaries that confined ocean peoples to tiny spaces for the first time. These boundaries today define the island states and territories of the Pacific. I have just used the term "ocean peoples" because our ancestors, who had lived in the Pacific for over two thousand years, viewed their world as "a sea of islands" rather than "islands in the sea." This may be seen in a common categorisation of people, as exemplified in Tonga by the inhabitants of the main, capital island, who used to refer to their compatriots from the rest of the archipelago not so much as "people from outer islands," as social scientists would say, but as *kakai mei tahi* or just *tahi:* "people from the sea." This characterisation reveals the underlying assumption that the sea is home to such people.

The difference between the two perspectives is reflected in the two terms used for our region: Pacific Islands and Oceania. The first term, "Pacific Islands," is the prevailing one used everywhere; it denotes small areas of land sitting atop submerged reefs or seamounts. Hardly any anglophone economist, consultancy expert, government planner, or development banker in the region uses the term "Oceania," perhaps because it sounds grand and somewhat romantic and may denote something so vast that it would compel them to a drastic review of their perspectives and policies. The French and other Europeans use the term "Oceania" to an extent that English-speakers, apart from the much-maligned anthropologists and a few other sea-struck scholars, have not. It may not be coincidental that Australia, New Zealand, and the United States, anglophone all, have far greater interests in the Pacific and how it is perceived than have the distant European nations.

"Oceania" denotes a sea of islands with their inhabitants. The world of our ancestors was a large sea full of places to explore, to make their homes in, to breed generations of seafarers like themselves. People raised in this environment were at home with the sea. They played in it as soon as they could walk steadily, they worked in it, they fought on it. They developed great skills for navigating their waters—as well as the spirit to traverse even the few large gaps that separated their island groups.

Theirs was a large world in which peoples and cultures moved and mingled, unhindered by boundaries of the kind erected much later by imperial powers. From one island to another they sailed to trade and to marry, thereby expanding social networks for greater flows of wealth. They travelled to visit relatives in a wide variety of natural and cultural surroundings, to quench their thirst for adventure, and even to fight and dominate.

Fiji, Samoa, Tonga, Niue, Rotuma, Tokelau, Tuvalu, Futuna, and Uvea formed a large exchange community in which wealth and people with their skills and arts circulated endlessly. From this community people ventured to the north and west, into Kiribati, the Solomon Islands, Vanuatu, and New Caledonia, which formed an outer arc of less intensive exchange. Evidence of this voyaging is provided by present-day settlements within Melanesia of descendants of these seafarers. (Only blind landlubbers would say that settlements like these, as well as those in New Zealand and Hawai'i, were made through accidental voyages by people who got blown off course—presumably while they were out fishing with their wives, children, pigs, dogs, and food-plant seedlings during a hurricane.) The Cook Islands and French Polynesia formed a community similar to that of their cousins to the west; hardy spirits from this community ventured southward and founded settlements in Aotearoa, while others went in the opposite direction to discover and inhabit the islands of Hawai'i. Also north of the equator is the community that was centred on Yap.

Melanesia is supposedly the most fragmented world of all: tiny communities isolated by terrain and at least one thousand languages. The truth is that large regions of Melanesia were integrated by trading and cultural exchange systems that were even more complex than those of Polynesia and Micronesia. Lingua francas and the fact that most Melanesians have always been multilingual (which is more than one can say about most Pacific Rim countries) make utter nonsense of the notion that they were (and still are) babblers of Babel. It was in the interest of imperialism—and is in the interest of neocolonialism—to promote this blatant misconception of Melanesia.[3]

Evidence of the conglomerations of islands with their economies and cultures is readily available in the oral traditions of the islands and, too, in blood ties that are retained today. The highest chiefs of Fiji, Samoa, and Tonga, for example, still maintain kin connections, forged centuries before Europeans entered the Pacific, in the days when boundaries were not imaginary lines in the ocean but points of entry that were constantly negotiated and even contested. The sea was open to anyone who could navigate a way through.

This was the kind of world that bred men and women with skills and courage that took them into the unknown, to discover and populate all the habitable islands east of the 130th meridian. The great fame that they have earned posthumously may have been romanticised, but it is solidly based on real feats that could have been performed only by those born and raised with an open sea as their home.

Nineteenth-century imperialism erected boundaries that led to the contraction of Oceania, transforming a once boundless world into the Pacific Island states and territories that we know today. People were confined to their tiny spaces, isolated from each other. No longer could they travel freely to do what they had done for centuries. They were cut off from their relatives abroad, from their far-flung sources of wealth and cultural enrichment. This is the historical basis of the view that our countries are small, poor, and isolated. It is true only insofar as people are still fenced in and quarantined.

This assumption is no longer tenable as far as the countries of central and western Polynesia are concerned; it may be untenable also of Micronesia. The rapid expansion of the world economy in the years since World War II may have intensified third-world dependency, as has been noted from certain vantage points at high-level academia, but it also had a liberating effect on the lives of ordinary people in Oceania, as it did in the Caribbean islands. The new economic reality made nonsense of artificial boundaries, enabling the people to shake off their confinement. They have since moved, by the tens of thousands, doing what their ancestors did in earlier times: enlarging their world, as they go, on a scale not possible before. Everywhere they go—to Australia, New Zealand, Hawai'i, the mainland United States, Canada, Europe, and elsewhere—they strike roots in new resource areas, securing employment and overseas family property, expanding kinship networks through which they circulate themselves, their relatives, their material goods, and their stories all across their ocean, and the ocean is theirs because it has always been their home. Social scientists may write of Oceania as a Spanish Lake, a British Lake, an American Lake, even a Japanese Lake. But we all know that only those who make the ocean their home, and love it, can really claim it as their own. Conquerors come, conquerors go, the ocean remains, mother only to her children. This mother has a big heart though; she adopts anyone who loves her.

The resources of Samoans, Cook Islanders, Niueans, Tokelauans, Tuvaluans, I-Kiribati, Fijians, Indo-Fijians, and Tongans are no longer confined to their national boundaries. They are located wherever these people are living, permanently or otherwise, as they were before the age of Western imperialism. One can see this any day at seaports and airports throughout the Central Pacific, where consignments of goods from homes abroad are unloaded as those of the homelands are loaded. Construction materials, agricultural machinery, motor vehicles, other heavy goods, and a myriad other things are sent from relatives abroad, while handicrafts, tropical fruits and root crops, dried marine creatures, kava, and other delectables are dispatched from the homelands. Although this flow of goods is generally not included in official statistics, much of the welfare of ordinary people of Oceania depends on an informal movement along ancient routes drawn in bloodlines invisible to the enforcers of the laws of confinement and regulated mobility.

The world of Oceania is neither tiny nor deficient in resources. It was so only as a condition of the colonial confinement that lasted less than a century in a history of millennia. Human nature demands space for free movement—and the larger the space the better it is for people. Islanders have broken out of their confinement, are moving around and away from their homelands, not so much because their countries are poor, but because they were unnaturally confined and severed from many of their traditional sources of wealth, and because it is in their blood to be mobile. They are once again enlarging their world, establishing new resource bases and expanded networks for circulation. Alliances are already being forged by an increasing number of Islanders with the *tangata whenua* of Aotearoa and will inevitably be forged with the Native Hawaiians. It is not inconceivable that if Polynesians ever get together, their two largest homelands will be reclaimed in one form or another. They have already made their presence felt in these homelands and have stamped indelible imprints on the cultural landscapes.

We cannot see these processes clearly if we confine our attention to things within national boundaries and to events at the upper levels of political economies and regional and international diplomacy. Only when we focus on what ordinary people are actually doing, rather than on what they should be doing, can we see the broader picture of reality. The world of Oceania may no longer include the heavens and the underworld, but it certainly encompasses the great cities of Australia, New Zealand, the United States, and Canada. It is within this expanded world that the extent of the people's resources must be measured.

In general, the living standards of Oceania are higher than those of most third-world societies. To attribute this merely to aid and remittances—misconstrued deliberately or otherwise as a form of dependence on rich countries' economies—is an unfortunate misreading of contemporary reality. Ordinary Pacific people depend for their daily existence much, much more on themselves and their kin, wherever they may be, than on anyone's largesse, which they believe is largely pocketed by the elite classes. The funds and goods that homes-abroad people send their homeland relatives belong to no one but themselves. They earn every cent through hard physical toil in the new locations that need and pay for their labour. They also participate in the manufacture of many of the goods they send home; they keep the streets and buildings of Auckland clean; they keep its transportation system running smoothly; they keep the suburbs of the western United States (including Hawai'i) trimmed, neat, green, and beautiful; and they have contributed much, much more than has been acknowledged.

Islanders in their homelands are not the parasites on their relatives abroad that misinterpreters of "remittances" would have us believe. Economists do not take account of the social centrality of the ancient practice of reciprocity—the core of all oceanic cultures. They overlook the fact that for everything homeland relatives receive, they reciprocate with goods they themselves produce, by maintaining ancestral roots and lands for everyone, homes with warmed hearths for travellers to return to permanently or to strengthen their bonds, their souls, and their identities before they move on again. This is not dependence but interdependence—purportedly the essence of the global system. To say that it is something else and less is not only erroneous but denies people their dignity.

What I have stated so far should already have provided sufficient response to the assertion that the islands are isolated. They clearly are not. Through developments in high technology, for example, communications and transportation systems are a vast improvement on what they were twenty years ago. These may be very costly by any standard, but they are available and they are used. Telecommunications companies are making fortunes out of lengthy conversations between breathless relatives thousands of miles apart.

But the islands are not connected only with regions of the Pacific Rim. Within Oceania itself people are once again circulating in increasing numbers and frequency. Regional organisations—intergovernmental, educational, religious, sporting, and cultural—are responsible for much of this mobility. The University of the South Pacific, with its highly mobile staff and student bodies comprising men, women, and youth from the twelve island countries that own it and from outside the Pacific, is an excellent example. Increasingly the older movers and shakers of the islands are being replaced by younger ones; and when they meet each other in Suva, Honiara, Apia, Vila, or any other capital city of the Pacific, they meet as friends, as people who have gone through the same place of learning, who have worked and played and prayed together.

The importance of our ocean for the stability of the global environment, for meeting a significant proportion of the world's protein requirements, for the production of certain marine resources in waters that are relatively clear of pollution, for the global reserves of mineral resources, among others, has been increasingly recognised and puts paid to the notion that Oceania is the hole in the doughnut. Together with our exclusive economic zones, the areas of the earth's surface that most of our countries occupy can no longer be called small. In this regard, Kiribati, the Federated States of Micronesia, and French Polynesia, for example, are among the largest countries in the world. The emergence of organisations such as SPACHEE (South Pacific Action Committee for Human Environment and Ecology), SPREP (South Pacific Regional Environment Programme), the Forum Fisheries Agency, and SOPAC (South Pacific Applied Geosciences Commission); of movements for a nuclear-free Pacific, the prevention of toxic waste disposal, and the ban on the wall-of-death fishing methods, with linkages to similar organisations and movements elsewhere; and the establishment at the University of the South Pacific of the Marine Science and Ocean Resources Management programmes, with linkages to fisheries and ocean resources agencies throughout the Pacific and beyond—all indicate that we could play a pivotal role in the protection and sustainable development of our ocean. No people on earth are more suited to be guardians of the world's largest ocean than those for whom it has been home for generations. Although this is a different issue from the ones I have focussed on for most of this essay, it is relevant to the concern for a far better future for us than has been prescribed and predicted. Our role in the protection and development of our ocean is no mean task; it is no less than a major contribution to the well-being of humanity. Because it could give us a sense of doing something not only worthwhile but noble, we should seize the moment with despatch.

The perpetrators of the smallness view of Oceania have pointed out quite correctly the need for each island state or territory to enter into appropriate forms of specialised production for the world market, the need to improve their management and marketing techniques, and so forth. But they have so focussed on bounded national economies at the macrolevel that they have overlooked or understated the significance of the other processes I have outlined here and have thereby swept aside the whole universe of Oceanian mores and just about all our potential for autonomy. The explanation seems clear: one way or another, nearly all of them are involved directly or indirectly in the fields of aided development and Pacific Rim geopolitics, for whose purposes it is necessary to portray our huge world in tiny, needy bits. To acknowledge the larger reality would be to undermine the prevailing view and frustrate certain agendas and goals of powerful interests. These perpetrators are therefore participants, as I was, in the belittlement of Oceania and, too, in the perpetuation of the neocolonial relationships of dependency that are still being played out in the rarefied circles of national politicians, bureaucrats, diplomats, and assorted experts and academics, while far beneath them exists another order: ordinary people who are busily and independently redefining their world in accordance with their perception of their own interests and their conception of where the future lies for their children and their children's children. Those who maintain that the people of Oceania live from day to day, not really caring for the long-term benefits, are unaware of the elementary truth known by most native Islanders: that they plan for generations, for the continuity and improvement of their families and kin groups.

As I watched the Big Island of Hawai'i expanding into and rising from the depths, I saw in it the future for Oceania, our sea of islands. That future lies in the hands of our own people, not of those who would prescribe for us, get us forever dependent and indebted, because they can see no way out.

At the Honolulu Airport, while waiting for my flight back to Fiji, I met an old friend, a Tongan who is twice my size and lives in Berkeley, California. He is not an educated man. He works on people's yards, trimming hedges and trees, and laying driveways and footpaths. But every three months or so he flies to Fiji, buys $8,000 to $10,000 worth of kava, takes it on the plane flying him back to California, and sells it from his home. He has never heard of dependency; if he were told of it, it would hold no real meaning for him. He told me in Honolulu that he was bringing a cooler full of T-shirts, some for the students at the university with whom he often stays when he comes to Suva, and the rest for his relatives in Tonga, where he goes for a week or so while his kava is gathered, pounded, and bagged in Fiji. He later fills the cooler with seafood to take back home to California, where he has two sons he wants to put through college. On one of his trips he helped me renovate a house that I had just bought. We like him because he is a good storyteller and is generous with his money and time, but mostly because he is one of us.

There are thousands like him, flying back and forth across national boundaries, the international dateline, and the equator, far above and completely undaunted by the deadly serious discourses below on the nature of the Pacific Century, the Asia-Pacific coprosperity sphere, and the dispositions of the post–cold war Pacific Rim, cultivating their ever-growing universe in their own ways, which is as it should be, for therein lies their independence. No one else would give it to them—or to us.

Oceania is vast, Oceania is expanding, Oceania is hospitable and generous, Oceania is humanity rising from the depths of brine and regions of fire deeper still, Oceania is us. We are the sea, we are the ocean, we must wake up to this ancient truth and together use it to overturn all hegemonic views that aim ultimately to confine us again, physically and psychologically, in the tiny spaces that we have resisted accepting as our sole appointed places and from which we have recently liberated ourselves. We must not allow anyone to belittle us again, and take away our freedom.

Notes

I would like to thank Marshall Sahlins for convincing me in the end that not all is lost and that the world of Oceania is quite bright despite appearances. This essay is based on lectures delivered at the University of Hawai'i at Hilo and the East-West Center, Honolulu, March/April 1993. Vijay Naidu and Eric Waddell read a draft of this essay and made very helpful comments. I am profoundly grateful to them for their support.

1. For geographic and cultural reasons I include Fiji in Polynesia. Fiji, how-

ever, is much bigger and better endowed with natural resources than all other tropical Polynesian entities together.

2. I owe much to Eric Waddell for these terms (pers. comm.).

3. I use the terms "Melanesia," "Polynesia," and "Micronesia" because they are already part of the cultural consciousness of the peoples of Oceania. Before the nineteenth century there was only a vast sea in which people mingled in ways that, despite the European-imposed threefold division, have blurred the boundaries even to this day. This important issue is, however, beyond the purview of this essay.

The Ocean in Us

> We sweat and cry salt water, so we know that the ocean is really in our blood.
>
> —Teresia Teaiwa

IN A PREVIOUS essay, I advanced the notion of a much enlarged world of Oceania that has emerged through the astounding mobility of our peoples in the last fifty years (Hau'ofa 1993). Most of us are part of this mobility, whether personally or through the movements of our relatives. This expanded Oceania is a world of social networks that crisscross the ocean all the way from Australia and New Zealand in the southwest to the United States and Canada in the northeast. It is a world that we have created largely through our own efforts and have kept vibrant and independent of the Pacific Islands world of official diplomacy and neocolonial dependency. In portraying this new Oceania I wanted to raise, especially among our emerging generations, the kind of consciousness that would help free us from the prevailing, externally generated definitions of our past, present, and future.

I wish now to take this issue further by suggesting the development of a substantial regional identity that is anchored in our common inheritance of a very considerable portion of Earth's largest body of water: the Pacific Ocean. The notion of an identity for our region is not new; through much of the latter half of the twentieth century people have tried to instill a strong sense of belonging to an islands region for the sake of sustained regional cooperation. So far these attempts have foundered on the reefs of our diversity, and on the requirements of international geopolitics, combined with assertions of narrow national self-interest on the part of our individual countries. I believe that a solid and effective regional identity can be forged and fostered. We have not been very successful in our attempts so far because, while fishing for the elusive school of tuna, we have lost sight of the ocean that surrounds and sustains us.

A common identity that would help us to act together for the advancement of our collective interests, including the protection of the ocean for the general good, is necessary for the quality of our survival in the so-called Pacific Century when, as we are told, important developments in the global economy will concentrate in huge regions that encircle us. As individual, colonially created, tiny countries acting alone, we could indeed "fall off the map" or disappear into the black hole of a gigantic pan-Pacific doughnut, as our perspicacious friends, the denizens of the National Centre for Development Studies in Canberra, are fond of telling us. But acting together as a region, for the interests of the region as a whole, and above those of our individual countries, we would enhance our chances for a reasonable survival in the century that is already dawning upon us. Acting in unison for larger purposes and for the benefit of the wider community could help us to become more open-minded, idealistic, altruistic, and generous, and less self-absorbed and corrupt, in the conduct of our public affairs than we are today. In an age when our societies are preoccupied with the pursuit of material wealth, when the rampant market economy brings out unquenchable greed and amorality in us, it is necessary for our institutions of learning to develop corrective mechanisms, such as the one proposed here, if we are to retain our sense of humanity and community.

An identity that is grounded in something as vast as the sea should exercise our minds and rekindle in us the spirit that sent our ancestors to explore the oceanic unknown and make it their home, our home. I would like to make it clear at the outset that I am not in any way suggesting cultural homogeneity for our region. Such a thing is neither possible nor desirable. Our diverse loyalties are much too strong for a regional identity ever to erase them. Besides, our diversity is necessary for the struggle against the homogenising forces of the global juggernaut. It is even more necessary for those of us who must focus on strengthening their ancestral cultures in their struggles against seemingly overwhelming forces in order to regain their lost sovereignty. The regional identity that I am concerned with is something additional to the other identities we already have, or will develop in the future, something that should serve to enrich our other selves.

The ideas for a regional identity that I express here have emerged from nearly twenty years of direct involvement with an institution that caters to many of the tertiary educational needs of most of the South Pacific Islands

Region and, increasingly, countries north of the equator as well. In a very real sense the University of the South Pacific is a microcosm of the region. Many aspects of its history, which began in 1968 in the era of decolonisation of island territories, mirror the developments in the regional communities it serves. The well-known diversity of social organisations, economies, and cultures of the region is reflected in a student population that comprises people from all twelve countries that own the university, as well as a sprinkling from other regions. This sense of diversity is heightened by daily interactions—between students themselves, among staff, and between staff and students—that take place on our main campus in Suva, and by staff visits to regional countries to conduct face-to-face instruction of our extension students, summer schools, research, and consultancy, and to perform other university duties.

Yet through these same interactions there has developed at our university an ill-defined sense of belonging to a Pacific Islands Region, of being Pacific Islanders. Because of its size, its on-campus residential arrangements for staff and students, and its spread, the university is the premier hatchery for the regional identity. Nevertheless the sense of diversity is much more palpable and tangible than that of a larger common identity; students identify themselves much more with their nationality, race, and personal friendships across the cultural divide than with the Pacific Islander identity. This is to be expected. Apart from primordial loyalties, students come to the university to obtain certificates for returning home to work for their respective countries. They do not come to the university in order ultimately to serve the region as such.

In the early years of the university's existence there was a concerted attempt to strengthen the common identity through the promotion of the Pacific Way as a unifying ideology. But the Pacific Way was a shallow ideology that was swept away by the rising tide of regional disunity in the 1980s. While promoting the Pacific Way the university was simultaneously sponsoring diversity through the support it gave to student cultural groups based on nationality and race. This support was manifest most clearly in the sponsorship given to Pacific Week, an annual festival during which students displayed, largely through music and dance, the cultural diversity of the region. The irony of promoting both the Pacific Way and the Pacific Week was lost in the hope that unity would somehow emerge from diversity. But any lasting sense of unity derived from the enjoyment of the variety of music and dances of the region was tenuous because no serious attempt was made to translate them or place them in their historical and social contexts. Audiences enjoyed the melodies, the rhythms, and the movements; everything else was mystery. There is also a complete absence in the university's curricula of any degree programme in Pacific studies. Anthropology, one of the basic disciplines for such a programme, is not even taught at our university.

The development of a clear regional identity within this university was also hampered by the introduction in the early 1980s of neo-Marxism, which, as a global movement, was quite hostile to any expression of localism and regionalism. According to this ideology, Pacific people were part of a worldwide class structure based on an international division of labour. Nationalism and regionalism were bourgeois attempts to prevent the international unity of the working classes. The demise of the Pacific Way through natural causes—and the disappearance of neo-Marxism as a direct result of the 1987 right-wing military coups in Fiji—removed from our campus discourses the ideologies that transcended cultural diversity. Pacific Week sputtered on for another ten years, as an affirmative expression of difference, with nothing concrete to counterbalance it.

Outside the University of the South Pacific, Pacific Islands regionalism, promoted by several other regional organisations, was facing parallel problems together with a considerable degree of confusion. Much of this could be traced back to the colonial period. For example, our region has come under a variety of names that reflect not only confusion about what we are but also the ways in which we have been slotted into pigeonholes or juggled around for certain purposes. The earliest general name for the region was the South Seas, which became virtually synonymous with Paradise—a false concept that we have failed to shed because it is used to promote the hospitality industry. When I grew up in Papua New Guinea in the 1940s we were still South Sea Islanders. We had not heard of the South Pacific or Pacific Islanders.

A much less common term for our region is Australasia, which is a combination of Australia and Asia, meaning south of Asia. According to the Concise Oxford Dictionary, it refers to Australia and the islands of the Southwest Pacific. The term implies that the islands are in Australia's orbit. Not infrequently, however, Australians refer to the region as their "backyard," the sort of area that has to be guarded against intrusions from behind.

Only after World War II did the term "South Pacific" come into general and popular use. It seems to have first spread through the Western Alliance's military terminology during the war and was popularised by James Michener's book, *Tales of the South Pacific,* and Rodgers and Hammerstein's hugely successful musical version of it. But the term is misleading. As used in our premier regional organisations, "South Pacific" comprises not just those islands that lie south of the equator; it covers the whole region, from the Marianas, deep in the North Pacific, to New Zealand in the south. Be that as it may, the term "South Pacific" has replaced South Seas, which today is confined almost totally to history books and old records.

Since the beginning of the postcolonial era the term "Pacific Islands Region" has emerged and is gradually replacing South Pacific as the descriptive name for our region. The South Pacific Region was a creation of the cold war era, and its significance was largely in relation to the security of Western interests in the Far East. The South Pacific Region clearly included Australia and New Zealand, but the term "Pacific Islands Region" excludes our larger neighbours and indicates more clearly than before the separation between us and them. This may reflect our contemporary political sovereignty, but in more recent times it has emerged to signify our declining importance to the West since the end of the cold war, as well as the progressive movement by our neighbours towards Asia. The South Pacific of the cold war, when our region was liberally courted by the West, is finished. Perhaps the best indication of this is the recommendation made at the last meeting of the South Pacific Conference to remove the term South Pacific from its secretariat, the South Pacific Commission. It will come as no surprise if the secretariat is renamed the Pacific Islands Commission or some other redesignation to be determined by the ever-shifting perceptions of what our region is or should be. Will the same change be made to the conference itself? And what of the South Pacific Forum or, for that matter, our very own University of the South Pacific? The point is this: as the Pacific Islands Region we are no longer as needed by others as we once were; we are now increasingly told to shape up or else. The Forum Secretariat has been radically downsized, and the headship of the South Pacific Commission has recently been taken over by a non–Pacific Islander for the first time in about three decades.

Two other terms that include our region are significant indicators of our progressive marginalisation. The first is Asia-Pacific Region—used by certain international agencies, such as those of the United Nations, to lump us together with hundreds of millions of Asians for the administration of services of various kinds. The other term is Asia Pacific Economic Cooperation (APEC), which covers the entire Pacific Rim but excludes the whole of the Pacific Islands region. Thus in the United Nations' Asia-Pacific Region we are an appendage (or perhaps the appendix) of Asia, and in APEC we do not exist. It should now be evident why our region is characterised as the "hole in the doughnut," an empty space. We should take careful note of this because if we do not exist for others, then we could in fact be dispensable.

This is not an exaggeration. Early in the twentieth century the people of Banaba were persuaded to give up their island to a phosphate-mining company for the benefit of the British Empire. In midcentury the inhabitants of Bikini were coaxed into giving up their island for atomic tests that would benefit all mankind. Both groups of people consented to the destruction of their inheritance largely because they had no choice. They are today among the world's displaced populations; those who benefited from their sacrifice have forgotten or are doing their best to forget their existence. What does this bode for us in the twenty-first century and beyond? Banaba and Bikini were not isolated cases. The latter part of the twentieth century has made it clear that ours is the only region in the world where certain kinds of experiment and exploitation can be undertaken by powerful nations with minimum political repercussions to themselves. Modern society is generating and accumulating vast quantities of waste matter that must in the near future be disposed of where there will be least resistance. It may well be that for the survival of the human species in the next millennium we in Oceania will be urged, in the way the people of Banaba and Bikini were urged, to give up our lands and seas.

The older terms for our region were coined before any sense of regionalism on our part arose. In Africa and the Middle East, regionalism emerged from the struggle for independence. In our part of the world, regionalism first emerged as a creation of colonialism to preempt the rise of revolutionary or even nonrevolutionary independence movements. This is the root of much of the problem of regionalism in the Pacific. We have not been able to define our world and ourselves without direct and often heavy external influences.

In summary, we could take our changing identities as a region over the last two hundred years as marking the different stages of our history. In the earliest stage of our interactions with the outside world, we were the South

Sea paradise of noble savages living in harmony with a bountiful nature; we were simultaneously lost and degraded souls to be pacified, Christianised, colonised, and civilised. Then we became the South Pacific Region of great importance for the security of Western interests in Asia. We were pampered by those whose real interests lay elsewhere and those who conducted dangerous experiments on our islands. We have passed through that stage into the Pacific Islands Region of naked, neocolonial dependency. Our erstwhile suitors are now creating with others along the rim of our ocean a new set of relationships that excludes us totally. Had this been happening elsewhere, our exclusion would not have mattered much. But in this instance we are physically located at the very centre of what is occurring around us. The development of APEC will affect our existence in fundamental ways whether we like it or not. We cannot afford to ignore our exclusion because what is involved here is our very survival.

The time has come for us to wake up to our modern history as a region. We cannot confront the issues of the Pacific Century individually, as tiny countries, nor as the Pacific Islands Region of bogus independence. We must develop a much stronger and genuinely independent regionalism than what we have today. A new sense of the region that is our own creation, based on our perceptions of our realities, is necessary for our survival in the dawning era.

Our present regionalism is a direct creation of colonialism. It emerged soon after World War II with the establishment—by Australia, France, Great Britain, the Netherlands, New Zealand, and the United States—of the South Pacific Conference and later its secretariat, the South Pacific Commission. The 1950 South Pacific Conference at Nasinu, Fiji, was the first occasion ever in which indigenous island leaders from throughout Oceania met in a single forum to discuss practical issues of common interest to them. The agenda, of course, was set by the colonial powers. These authorities dominated the conference and the commission, which they had established to facilitate the pooling of resources and the effective implementation of regional programmes in health, education, agriculture, fisheries, and so forth, and to involve island leaders in the consideration of regional development policies. But behind all this was our rulers' attempt to present a progressive face to the United Nations decolonisation committee and to unite the region, under their leadership, in the struggle against Marxism and liberation ideologies. It is not surprising, then, that unlike other colonial regions of the world, our political independence (except in Vanuatu and Western Samoa) was largely imposed on us. It also came in packages that tied us firmly to the West.

Politics was not discussed in the South Pacific Conference, a policy that has survived more or less in regional organisations that have emerged in the postcolonial period. Although the Nasinu conference and subsequent South Pacific Conferences engendered a sense of regional identity, the ban on political discussions—which, at the time, concerned the burning issues of decolonisation and communist expansionism—prevented the development of this identity beyond a vague sense of commonality.

The frustration with external domination of the South Pacific Conference led to the formation of the South Pacific Forum as an exclusive club by the leaders of the newly independent countries of the region. But the independence of the South Pacific Forum was compromised from the beginning with the inclusion, for financial considerations, of Australia and New Zealand in its membership. The membership of these countries in the South Pacific Conference and the South Pacific Forum has brought about complications in the development of a postcolonial regional identity. Australia and New Zealand are members of these regional bodies not as nations but as patron governments. By mutual identification, their leaders who attend high-level regional meetings, and their representatives in regional secretariats, do not call themselves nor are they considered Pacific Islanders. They are, however, our closest neighbours, with whom we have had historical and cultural connections that date back to the beginning of the European settlements of their countries. There is already an identity with these countries based on history, geography, and numerous contemporary involvements, but this is fraught with ambivalence. New Zealand and especially Australia are not infrequently considered by us to be domineering, exploitative, and in possession of the gentleness and sensitivity of the proverbial bull in a china shop, while we are often considered by the other side to be mendicant and mendacious and our leading citizens woefully inept. Among ourselves, we do hold and express mutually uncomplimentary views and occasionally act violently against each other—attitudes and conduct that are inimical to the development of regionalism. The point, however, is that by virtue of their governments' membership in our premier regional organisations, Australia and New Zealand exert strong, if not dominant, influences in the conduct of our regional affairs and in the shaping of any Pacific Islands identity. At the same time these countries display a strong chameleonic tendency; they have a habit of dropping in and out of the South Pacific region whenever it suits their national self-interest.

National self-interest and pride, the emergence of subregional blocks based on perceived cultural and ethnic affiliations, the timidity and sheer lack of foresight on the part of our leaders—all are instances of numerous problems that beset Pacific Islands regionalism. Since these are commonly known, I will not discuss them here; suffice it to say that in general our regional organisations exist today mainly to serve national interests rather than those of the region as such.

Nevertheless, in the few instances when the region stood united, we have been successful in achieving our common aims. It is of utmost significance for the strengthening of a regional identity to know that our region has achieved its greatest degree of unity on issues involving threats to our common environment: the ocean. It should be noted that on these issues Australia and New Zealand have often assumed the leading roles because of our common sharing of the ocean. On issues of this kind the sense of a regional identity, of being Pacific Islanders, is felt most acutely. The movement towards a nuclear-free and independent Pacific, the protests against the wall-of-death drift-netting, against plans to dispose of nuclear waste in the ocean, the incineration of chemical weapons on Johnston Island, the 1995 resumption of nuclear tests on Moruroa, and, most ominously, the spectre of our atoll islands and low-lying coastal regions disappearing under the rising sea level—all are instances of a regional united front against threats to our environment. But as these issues come to the fore only occasionally, and as success in protesting has dissipated the immediate sense of threat, we have generally reverted to our normal state of disunity and the pursuit of national self-indulgence. The problems, especially those of toxic waste disposal and destructive exploitation of ocean resources, remain to haunt us. Nuclear-powered ships and vessels carrying radioactive materials still ply the ocean; international business concerns are still looking for islands for the disposal of toxic industrial wastes; activities that contribute to the depletion of the ozone continue; drift-netting has abated but not stopped; and the reefs of Moruroa Atoll may still crack and release radioactive materials. People who are concerned with these threats are trying hard to enlist regionwide support, but the level of their success has been modest. Witness the regionwide silence while the plutonium-laden *Pacific Teal* sailed through our territorial waters in March 1997. There is, however, a trend in the region to move from mere protest to the stage of active protection of the environment. For this to succeed, regionalism has to be strengthened. No single country in the Pacific can by itself protect its own slice of the oceanic environment: the very nature of that environment prescribes regional effort. And to develop the ocean resources sustainably, regional unity is required.

A Pacific Islands regional identity means a Pacific Islander identity. What or who is a Pacific Islander? The University of the South Pacific categorises its students and staff into regionals and nonregionals. A regional is someone who is a citizen of one of the member countries of the university's region. A regional is a Pacific Islander. But the issue is more complex than that. There are thousands of people with origins in Oceania who are citizens of Canada, the United States, Australia, and New Zealand and who consider themselves Pacific Islanders. In Fiji about half the citizen population is of nonindigenous origin, and they are not considered or called Fijians. The term Fijian is reserved for the indigenous population, which still considers the rest as *vulagi,* or guests, even though their ancestors might have emigrated to Fiji a century or so ago. Fijians are Pacific Islanders. What of the rest? Given the mutual misunderstandings and suspicions between indigenous Fijians and to some extent most other indigenous Pacific Islanders on the one hand, and Indo-Fijians on the other, what proportion of the latter consider themselves Pacific Islanders? The view held by some people in the region is that only indigenous populations are Pacific Islanders. One of the reasons why many people disliked the Pacific Way ideology was their perceived exclusion from its coverage. There were (and perhaps still are) a few people in Tonga with full or part foreign ancestry who were (or still are) stateless persons. Cook Islanders are citizens of their own country and simultaneously of New Zealand. French Polynesians and New Caledonians are French citizens; Guamanians are American citizens; American Samoans have one leg in the United States and the other in Eastern Samoa. To what degree are these people Pacific Islanders? Similar questions could be raised about the New Zealand Maori, Native Hawaiians, and Australian Aborigines.

In anticipation of what I shall say later, I would like to make one point briefly. The issue of what or who is a Pacific Islander would not arise if we considered Oceania as comprising people—as human beings with a common heritage and commitment—rather than as members of diverse nationalities and races. Oceania refers to a world of people connected to each other. The term Pacific Islands Region refers to an official world of states and nationalities. John and Mary cannot just be Pacific Islanders; they have to be Ni-Vanuatu, or Tuvaluan, or Samoan first. As far as I am concerned, anyone who has lived in our region and is committed to Oceania is an Oceanian. This view opens up the possibility of expanding Oceania progressively to cover larger areas and more peoples than is possible under the term Pacific Islands Region. In this formulation, the concepts Pacific Islands Region and Pacific Islanders are as redundant as South Seas and South Sea Islanders. We have to search for appropriate names for common identities that are more accommodating, inclusive, and flexible than what we have today.

At our university, the search for unity and common identity took on a new life following two incidents of violent confrontation in 1994 between inebriated students of different nationalities. In the aftermath of these incidents, which shook the university to its foundations, renewed efforts were made to bring about a sense of unity and common identity among our students in order to promote cross-cultural understanding and cooperation and to forestall further outbreaks of violence. Measures were taken to minimise the deleterious consequences of diversity. Funding of cultural groups was drastically reduced, Pacific Week was abandoned, and the flag-raising ceremonies to celebrate national days were discontinued. Students were urged to regroup themselves into interest-based associations with memberships that cut across nationality and ethnicity. Our staff reexamined our academic programmes, resulting in the introduction of a common course in Pacific studies, which itself is the beginning of a drive to introduce a Pacific studies degree programme for the first time—at this university of all places. In 1996, the university finally acted on a decision made by its council in 1992 to establish an arts and culture programme by creating a centre for Pacific arts and culture, which opened in 1997.

As I was intimately involved in the planning for this centre, which deals directly with the issue of culture and identity, I became aware of two things. First, this new unit provides a rare opportunity for some of us at the university to realise the dreams we have had for many years. We have talked and written about our ideas and hopes, but only now have we been presented with an opportunity to transform them into reality. Second, if we were not careful, the programmes being conceived for the centre would become a loose collection of odds and ends that would merely reflect the diversity of our cultures.

I began searching for a theme or a central concept on which to hang the programmes of the centre. I toyed with the idea of Our Sea of Islands, which

I had propounded a few years earlier, but felt uneasy about it because I did not wish to appear to be conspicuously riding a hobbyhorse. It is bad manners in many Oceanian societies to appear pushy. You do not push things for yourself. But it is a forgivable sin if you accidentally get someone else to do it for you. So I kept the idea at the back of my mind, and while in this condition I came across the following passage in an article written by Sylvia Earle for *Time Magazine* in 1996:

> The sea shapes the character of this planet, governs weather and climate, stabilizes moisture that falls back on the land, replenishing Earth's fresh water to rivers, lakes, streams—and us. Every breath we take is possible because of the life-filled life-giving sea; oxygen is generated there, carbon dioxide absorbed. Both in terms of the sheer mass of living things and genetic diversity, that's where the action is.
>
> Rain forests and other terrestrial systems are important too, of course, but without the living ocean there would be no life on land. Most of Earth's living space, the biosphere, is ocean—about 97%. And not so coincidentally 97% of Earth's water is Ocean.

After I read Earle's account, it became clear that the ocean, and our historical relationship with it, would be the core theme for the centre. At about the same time, our journalism students produced the first issue of their newspaper, *Wansolwara,* a pidgin word that they translated as "one ocean, one people." Things started to fall into place, and we were able to persuade the university to call the new unit the Oceania Centre for Arts and Culture. It also occurred to me that despite the sheer magnitude of the oceans, we are among the minute proportion of Earth's total human population who can truly be referred to as "oceanic peoples." Besides, our region is sometimes referred to as Oceania, a designation that I prefer above all others for some very good reasons.

All our cultures have been shaped in fundamental ways by the adaptive interactions between our people and the sea that surrounds our island communities. In general, the smaller the island the more intensive the interactions with the sea—and the more pronounced the sea's influence on culture. One did not have to be in direct interaction with the sea to be influenced by it. Regular climatic patterns, together with such unpredictable natural phenomena as droughts, prolonged rains, floods, and cyclones that influenced the systems of terrestrial activities, were largely determined by the ocean.

On the largest island of Oceania, New Guinea, products of the sea, especially the much-valued shells, reached the most remote highlands societies, shaping their ceremonial and political systems. But more important, inland people of our large islands are now citizens of Oceanian countries whose capitals and other urban centres are located in coastal areas, to which they are moving in large numbers to seek advancement. The sea is already part of their lives. Many of us today are not directly or personally dependent on the sea for our livelihood and would probably get seasick as soon as we set foot on a rocking boat. This means only that we are no longer sea travellers or fishers. But as long as we live on our islands we remain very much under the spell of the sea; we cannot avoid it.

Before the advent of Europeans in our region, our cultures were truly oceanic in the sense that the sea barrier shielded us for millennia from the great cultural influences that raged through continental landmasses and adjacent islands. This prolonged period of isolation allowed for the emergence of distinctive oceanic cultures with no nonoceanic influences—except on the original cultures that the earliest settlers brought with them when they entered the vast, uninhabited region. Scholars of antiquity may raise the issue of continental cultural influences on the western and northwestern border islands of Oceania, but these are exceptions, and Asian mainland influences were largely absent until the modern era. On the eastern extremity of the region there were some influences from the Americas, but these were minimal. For these reasons Pacific Ocean islands, from Japan through the Philippines and Indonesia, which are adjacent to the Asian mainland, do not have oceanic cultures and are therefore not part of Oceania. This definition of our region that delineates us clearly from Asia and the pre-Columbian Americas is based on our own historical developments rather than on other people's perceptions of us.

Although the sea shielded us from Asian and American influence, the nature of the spread of our islands allowed a great deal of mobility within the region. The sea provided waterways that connected neighbouring islands into regional exchange groups that tended to merge into one another, allowing the diffusion of cultural traits through most of Oceania. These common traits of bygone and changing traditions have so far provided many of the elements for the construction of regional identities. But many people on our islands do not share these common traits as part of their heritage, and an increasing number of true urbanites are alienated from their ancient histories. In other words: although our historical and cultural traditions are important elements of a regional identity, they are not in themselves sufficient to sustain that identity for they exclude all those people whose ancestral heritage is sourced elsewhere and those who are growing up in nontraditional environments.

The ocean that surrounds us is the one physical entity that all of us in Oceania share. It is the inescapable fact of our lives. What we lack is the conscious awareness of it, its implications, and what we could do with it. The potentials are enormous, exciting—as they have always been. When our leaders and planners say that our future lies in the sea, they are thinking only in economic terms: about marine and seabed resources and their development. When people talk of the importance of the oceans for the continuity of life on Earth, they are making scientific statements. But for us in Oceania, the sea defines us, what we are and have always been. As the great Caribbean poet Derek Walcott put it, the sea is history. Recognition of this could be the beginning of a very important chapter in our history. We could open it as we enter the third millennium.

All of us in Oceania today, whether indigenous or otherwise, can truly assert that the sea is our single common heritage. Because the ocean is everflowing, the sea that laps the coastlines of Fiji, for example, is the same water that washes the shores of all the other countries of our region. Most of the dry land surfaces on our islands have been divided and allocated, and conflicting claims to land rights are the roots of some of the most intractable problems in virtually all our communities. Until very recently, the sea beyond the horizon and the reefs that skirt our islands was open water that belonged to no one and everyone. Much of the conflict between the major ethnic groups in Fiji, for example, is rooted in the issue of land rights. But the open sea beyond the nearshore areas of indigenous Fijian fishing rights is open to every Fiji citizen and free of dispute. Similarly, as far as ordinary people of Oceania are concerned, there are no national boundaries drawn across the sea between our countries. Just about every year, for example, some lost Tongan fishers, who might well have been fishing in Fijian waters, wash up in their frail vessels on the shores of Fiji. They have always been taken very good care of, then flown back home loaded with tinned fish.

It is one of the great ironies of the Law of the Sea Convention, which enlarged our national boundaries, that it is also extending the territorial instinct to where there was none before. As we all know, territoriality is probably the strongest spur for brutal acts of aggression. Because of the resource potentials of the open sea and the ocean bed, the water that united subregions of Oceania in the past may become a major divisive factor in the relationships between our countries in the future. It is therefore essential that we ground any new regional identity in a belief in the common heritage of the sea. Simple recognition that the ocean is uncontainable and pays no respect to territoriality should goad us to advance the notion, based on physical reality and practices that date back to the initial settlement of Oceania, that the sea must remain open to all of us.

A regional identity anchored in our common heritage of the ocean does not mean an assertion of exclusive regional territorial rights. The water that washes and crashes on our shores is the water that washes and crashes on the coastlines of the whole Pacific Rim from Antarctica to New Zealand, Australia, Southeast and East Asia, and right around to the Americas. The Pacific Ocean also merges into the Atlantic and the Indian Oceans to encircle the entire planet. Just as the sea is an open and ever-flowing reality, so should our oceanic identity transcend all forms of insularity, to become one that is openly searching, inventive, and welcoming. In a metaphorical sense the ocean that has been our waterway to each other should also be our route to the rest of the world. Our most important role should be that of custodians of the ocean; as such we must reach out to similar people elsewhere in the common task of protecting the seas for the general welfare of all living things. This may sound grandiose but it really is not, considering the growing importance of international movements to implement the most urgent projects in the global environmental agenda: protection of the ozone layer, the forests, and the oceans. The formation of an oceanic identity is really an aspect of our waking up to things that are already happening around us.

The ocean is not merely our omnipresent, empirical reality; equally important, it is our most wonderful metaphor for just about anything we can think of. Contemplation of its vastness and majesty, its allurement and fickleness, its regularities and unpredictability, its shoals and depths, its isolating and linking role in our histories—all this excites the imagination and kindles a sense of wonder, curiosity, and hope that could set us on journeys to explore new regions of creative enterprise that we have not dreamt of before.

What I have tried to say so far is that in order to give substance to a common regional identity and animate it, we must tie history and culture to empirical reality and practical action. This is not new; our ancestors wrote our histories on the landscape and the seascape; carved, stencilled, and wove our metaphors on objects of utility; and sang and danced in rituals and ceremonies for the propitiation of the awesome forces of nature and society.

Some thirty years ago, Albert Wendt, in his landmark paper "Towards a New Oceania," wrote of his vision of the region and its first season of postcolonial cultural flowering. The first two paragraphs read:

> I belong to Oceania—or, at least, I am rooted in a fertile portion of it—and it nourishes my spirit, helps to define me, and feeds my imagination. A detached/objective analysis I will leave to sociologists and all the other 'ologists.' . . . Objectivity is for such uncommitted gods. My commitment won't allow me to confine myself to so narrow a vision. So vast, so fabulously varied a scatter of islands, nations, cultures, mythologies and myths, so dazzling a creature, Oceania deserves more than an attempt at mundane fact; only the imagination in free flight can hope—if not to contain her—to grasp some of her shape, plumage, and pain.
>
> I will not pretend that I know her in all her manifestations. No one . . . ever did; no one does . . . ; no one ever will because whenever we think we have captured her she has already assumed new guises—the love affair is endless, even her vital statistics . . . will change endlessly. In the final instance, our countries, cultures, nations, planets are what we imagine them to be. One human being's reality is another's fiction. Perhaps we ourselves exist only in one another's dreams. [1976, 49]

At the end of his rumination on the cultural revival in Oceania, partly through the words of the region's first generation of postcolonial writers and poets, Wendt concluded with this remark (1976, 60): "This artistic renaissance is enriching our cultures further, reinforcing our identities/self-respect/and pride, and taking us through a genuine decolonisation; it is also acting as a unifying force in our region. In their individual journeys into the Void, these artists, through their work, are explaining us to ourselves and creating a new Oceania."

This is very true. And for a new Oceania to take hold it must have a solid dimension of commonality that we can perceive with our senses. Culture and nature are inseparable. The Oceania that I see is a creation of countless people in all walks of life. Artists must work with others, for creativity lies in all fields, and besides we need each other.

These were the thoughts that went through my mind as I searched for a thematic concept on which to focus a sufficient number of programmes to give the Oceania Centre a clear, distinctive, and unifying identity. The theme for the centre and for us to pursue is the ocean and, as well, the interactions between us and the sea that have shaped and are shaping so much of our cultures. We begin with what we have in common and draw inspiration from the diverse patterns that have emerged from the successes and failures in our adaptation to the influences of the sea. From there we can range beyond the tenth horizon, secure in the knowledge of the home base to which we will always return for replenishment and revision of the purposes and directions of our journeys. We shall visit our people who have gone to the lands of diaspora and tell them that we have built something: a new home for all of us. And taking a cue from the ocean's ever-flowing and encircling nature, we will travel far and wide to connect with oceanic and maritime peoples elsewhere, and swap stories of voyages we have taken and those yet to be embarked on. We will show them what we have created; we will learn from them different kinds of music, dance, art, ceremonies, and other forms of cultural production. We may even together make new sounds, new rhythms, new choreographies, and new songs and verses about how wonderful and terrible the sea is, and how we cannot live without it. We will talk about the good things the oceans have bestowed on us, the damaging things we have done to them, and how we must together try to heal their wounds and protect them forever.

I have said elsewhere that no people on earth are more suitable to be the custodians of the oceans than those for whom the sea is home. We seem to have forgotten that we are such a people. Our roots, our origins, are embedded in the sea. All our ancestors, including those who came as recently as sixty years ago, were brought here by the sea. Some were driven here by war, famine, and pestilence; some were brought by necessity, to toil for others; and some came seeking adventures and perhaps new homes. Some arrived in good health, others barely survived the traumas of passage. For whatever reasons, and through whatever experiences they endured, they came by sea to the Sea, and we have been here since. If we listened attentively to stories of ocean passage to new lands, and of the voyages of yore, our minds would open up to much that is profound in our histories, to much of what we are and what we have in common.

Contemporary developments are taking us away from our sea anchors. Most of our modern economic activities are land based. We travel mostly by air, flying miles above the oceans, completing our journeys in hours instead of days and weeks and months. We rear and educate our young on things that have scant relevance to the sea. Yet we are told that the future of most of our countries lies there. Have we forgotten so much that we will not easily find our way back to the ocean?

As a region we are floundering because we have forgotten, or spurned, the study and contemplation of our pasts, even our recent histories, as irrelevant for the understanding and conduct of our contemporary affairs. We have thereby allowed others who are well equipped with the so-called objective knowledge of our historical development to continue reconstituting and reshaping our world and our selves with impunity, and in accordance with their shifting interests at any given moment in history. We have tagged along with this for so long that we have kept our silence even though we have virtually been defined out of existence. We have floundered also because we have considered regionalism mainly from the points of view of individual national interests rather than the interest of a wider collectivity. And we have failed to build any clear and enduring regional identity—partly because so far we have constructed edifices with disconnected traits from traditional cultures and passing events, edifices without concrete foundations.

The regional identity proposed here has been built on a base of concrete reality. That the sea is as real as you and I, that it shapes the character of this planet, that it is a major source of our sustenance, that it is something we all share in common wherever we are in Oceania—all are statements of fact. But above that level of everyday experience, the sea is our pathway to each other and to everyone else, the sea is our endless saga, the sea is our most powerful metaphor, the ocean is in us.

Note

This essay is based on one that was delivered as an Oceania Lecture at the University of the South Pacific, Suva, on 12 March 1997 and subsequently published in *Dreadlocks in Oceania* 1 (1997):124–148. A briefer, earlier version was delivered as a keynote address at the Third Conference of the European Society of Oceanists, Copenhagen, 13–15 December 1996. I am grateful to Greg Fry for his very insightful papers, "Framing the Islands," "The Politics of South Pacific Regional Cooperation," and "The South Pacific 'Experiment'." Our recent conversation in Wainadoi helped to clarify a number of issues dealt with here.

References

Earle, Sylvia. 1996. "The Well of Life." *Time Magazine,* 28 October.

Fry, Greg. 1991. "The Politics of South Pacific Regional Cooperation." In *The South Pacific: Problems, Issues, Prospects,* edited by Ramesh Thakur. London: Macmillan/University of Otago.

———. 1997a. "Framing the Islands: Knowledge and Power in Changing Australian Images of 'the South Pacific'." *Contemporary Pacific* 9:305–344.

———. 1997b. "The South Pacific 'Experiment': Reflections on the Origins of Regional Identity." *Journal of Pacific History* 32 (2):180–202.

Hau'ofa, Epeli. 1993. "Our Sea of Islands." In *A New Oceania: Rediscovering Our Sea of Islands,* edited by Eric Waddell, Vijay Naidu, and Epeli Hau'ofa. Suva: School of Social and Economic Development, University of the South Pacific. Reprinted in *Contemporary Pacific* 6 (1994):147–161.

Wendt, Albert. 1976. "Towards a New Oceania." *Mana Review* 1:49–60. Reprinted in *Seaweeds and Constructions* 7 (1983):71–85.

Pasts to Remember

> Shatrugun spots the boy in the crowd; he is standing under a breadfruit tree at a distance from the watchers. All at once his hair turns to resin, his arms become boughs and his feet sprout roots that are driven miles into the earth. . . . Drive your roots deep enough and you end up in infinity, says the breadfruit tree. . . . But infinity does not nourish, retorts the boy-tree, and promptly withdraws his roots to a patch of land beneath the breadfruit tree. And then his roots are too close to the surface and he reverts to the condition of a boy-farmer with feet, and is instantly seasick.
>
> —Sudesh Mishra in *Lila*

IN AN EARLIER publication (1993), I offered a view of ourselves that is more optimistic than the currently prevailing notions of our present and future as peoples of Oceania. That view is tied to my firmly held belief that all social realities are human creations—and that if we fail to construct our own realities other people will do it for us. It can be said that this concern is much ado about nothing. I wish that this were true, but it is not. People with powerful connections have presented us in certain ways that have influenced our self-perceptions and the ways in which we have been perceived and treated by others. Sir Thomas Davis, former prime minister of the Cook Islands, was a prominent Pacific Islands regional leader in the 1970s and 1980s. In his book *Island Boy,* he offers a telling statement of what could happen when we accept other people's representations of us:

> Because we believed it when we were told that small Pacific Islands States could never make a go of it without largesse from their former colonial masters, we did not try very hard to see the possibilities from our own points of view which had to be quite different from theirs [Australians' and New Zealanders']. . . . We, therefore, accepted largesse as a right, without questioning

the matter any further, and without the thought that some day it may not be forthcoming. [1992, 305]

As I said at the beginning, I have tried to deal with aspects of our present and future. I propose now to look into our past. I believe that in order for us to gain greater autonomy than we have today and maintain it within the global system, we must in addition to other measures be able to define and construct our pasts and present in our own ways. We cannot continue to rely on others to do it for us because autonomy cannot be attained through dependence.

Intermittently in the 1980s and through to the very early 1990s, I followed the discussions of ideas propounded by certain anthropologists about the constructions of the past and the politics of culture.[1] What these cultural constructionists are doing is what we have been doing all along—that is, constructing our pasts, our histories, from vast storehouses of narratives, both written and oral, to push particular agendas. One of the more positive aspects of our existence in Oceania is that truth is flexible and negotiable, despite attempts by some of us to impose political, religious, and other forms of absolutism. Versions of truth may be accepted for particular purposes and moments, only to be reversed when circumstances demand other versions; and we often accede to things just to stop being bombarded, and then go ahead and do what we want to do anyway.

But cultural constructionists of a certain persuasion have gone beyond the bounds by arrogating to themselves the role of final arbiters of what is true or false in our societies: true history, false history; genuine culture, spurious culture. It is a new hegemony, or perhaps it is the old one in a new guise. Our chiefs and other leaders have been doing it, but we have ways of dealing with this sort of thing. Our freedom lies in the flexibility in all kinds of discourses on the nature of our societies and on the directions of our development. There are no final truths or falsehoods, only interpretations, temporary consensus, and even impositions, for particular purposes. Cultural constructionists aim to control and direct our discourses on our own affairs, which is unwarranted. It is also potentially dangerous, for these scholars could be politically influential, as Haunani-Kay Trask (1991) has asserted.

Until recent years with the rise into prominence of historical anthropology and ethnographic history, there has been a near-total domination of the scholarly reconstructions of our pasts by the Canberra school of Pacific historians. From their works we can see that fundamental to the conceptualisation and writing of our histories is the division of our past into two main periods: the precontact and postcontact periods. The determining factor for this is the presence of Europeans with their traditions of writing and recording. Many years ago, while visiting a rural community in Papua New Guinea, I was invaded by a particularly virulent kind of lice. Some people call them crab lice, but these looked more like giant lobsters. I went to a nearby hospital run by a group of missionary sisters, one of whom told me in a serious and concerned manner to be very careful, for any slight body contact with the local inhabitants would cause much misery. Since then I have always associated the word "contact" with nasty infections. As used by historians and other scholars the term is very apt; it describes accurately the first and early encounters between Oceanians and European sailors as carriers of dangerous diseases that wiped out large proportions of our populations in the eighteenth and nineteenth centuries. Within one hundred years the indigenous population of Hawai'i, for example, was reduced by more than ninety percent. There was a real concern towards the end of the nineteenth century that we would vanish from the face of the earth because of such rampaging diseases. Ironically, a major concern in the twilight years of the twentieth century was that there were too many of us around.

Marxist sociologists, who began arriving at our university in the early 1980s, would not use the term "contact" because of its capitalist association. Instead they introduced a beautiful substitute, "penetration," as in "capitalist penetration of the Pacific" or "get penetrated." This is also a very apt term for it connotes consummation without mutual consent. We should get rid of these words and use better ones like "meet," "encounter," and so on.

The point is that for Pacific scholars the main factors for the reconstruction of our pasts are events determined by Euro-American imperialism. Our histories are commonly structured on the temporal division of the past into precontact, early contact, colonial, and postcolonial or neocolonial periods. In this formulation, Oceania has no history before imperialism, only what is called "prehistory": before history. In many if not most of our history books, more than nine-tenths of the period of our existence in Oceania is cramped into a chapter or two on prehistory and perhaps indigenous social organisation. These comprise a brief prelude to the real thing: history beginning with the arrival of Europeans. As it is, our histories are essentially narratives told in the footnotes of the histories of empires.

For those of us who want to reconstruct our remote and recent pasts in our own images—for the purpose of attaining and maintaining cultural autonomy and resisting the continuing encroachments on and domination of our lives by global forces aided and abetted by comprador institutions—this kind of history is a hindrance. Although it is very useful, even essential, for the understanding of vital aspects of our heritage, it is a hindrance in that it marginalises our peoples by relegating them to the roles of spectators and objects for transformation into good Christians, democrats, bureaucrats, commercial producers, cheap labourers, and the like. It does not see them as major players in the shaping of their histories. The main actors are explorers, early traders, missionaries, planters, colonial officials, and so forth.

Pacific histories also marginalise almost all our pasts by considering them not history, merely prehistory, to be dealt with by folklorists and a dwindling number of archaeologists and linguists. It can be argued that we really do have no history before imperialism. I cannot accept that, because we can argue that the much maligned oral narratives are as reliable or unreliable, biased or unbiased, as are written documents for sourcing history. We do know that all sources are contestable; otherwise history is complete and closed, which is nonsense. Every generation rewrites its history, as the saying goes. Besides, mainline history is only one way of reconstructing the past, which has no existence without reference to the present. How one reconstructs the past, as history or whatever, is a political act—a choice from valid alternatives made for particular purposes.

When you view most of a people's past as not history, you shorten very drastically the roots of their culture or even declare their existence doubtful. It is not surprising, then, that many academics hold the view that the peoples and cultures of Oceania are inventions of imperialism. This view has attained the status of truth only because people have been sidelined from their histories and conceptually severed from most of their pasts. It has been used to frustrate our endeavours to attain autonomy by characterising most of what we say or do as being borrowed from the "dominant culture"—as if borrowing is unique to us. As far as I know, our cultures have always been hybrid and hybridising, for we have always given to and taken from our neighbours and others we encounter; but the "dominant culture" is undoubtedly the most hybrid of all, for it has not just borrowed but looted unconscionably the treasures of cultures the world over. Like cultural constructionism, the prevailing Pacific historiography is hegemonic. With only minor concessions it admits of no other than mainline historiography.

Having identified the problem, we may ask: Where do we go from here? What should we do? If we are to go beyond adding our viewpoints to history as usual, we have to devise other methods, using our own categories as much as possible for producing our histories, our cultures. We could learn from the works of ethnographic historians and historical anthropologists, as well as from mainline historians, but we Oceanians must find ways of reconstructing our pasts that are our own. Non-Oceanians may construct and interpret our pasts or our present, but those are their constructions and interpretations, not ours. Theirs may be excellent and very instructive, but we must rely much more on ours. The rest of this chapter suggests some ideas for getting the ball rolling.

We may begin with delineating a new temporal dimension of history by doing away with the division of the past in which most of it lies outside history. Our histories did not begin with the coming of Europeans. If we continue to rely mainly on the works of archaeologists, linguists, botanists, zoologists, and the like for the reconstruction of our remote pasts, we will still be trapped with our pasts as prehistory. We must resort very seriously to our ecologically based oral narratives. Most historians, nurtured on written records and other kinds of concrete documentation as their primary sources, are leery of oral narratives, which they take to be free-floating tales disconnected from the physical world, impossible of verification, and therefore outside their purview.

A few years ago I came across the work of an Oceanian historical anthropologist, 'Okusitino Māhina, who argued very strongly that ecologically based oral traditions are as valid sources for "academic history" as are written documents (see Māhina 1992). As I read Māhina's work, which is an entire history based largely on oral traditions backed wherever possible with the findings of archaeology and related disciplines, it dawned on me that here in the making was a new Pacific historiography by an Oceanian scholar. A few historians may be working along similar lines, but it is significant that Māhina's background is anthropology, the discipline that has spearheaded the rethinking of Pacific historiography. The point at issue here is whether there are legitimate histories apart from mainline history. If there are, and I believe that there are, then our histories are as old as our remembered pasts.

Human events occur as interactions between people in time and space. First we look at people. In our reconstructions of Pacific histories of the recent past, for example, we must clear the stage and bring in new characters. We bring to the centre stage, as main players, our own peoples and institutions. For this purpose we lay to rest once and for all the ghost of Captain Cook. This is not a suggestion to excise him entirely from our histories—far from it. Others, especially in New Zealand and Australia, will still consider him a superstar, so he will be looming large on the horizon. As for us, we merely send Captain Cook to the wings to await our summons when it is necessary to call in the Plague, and we may recall him at the end to take a bow. As long as this particular spirit struts the centre stage, our peoples and institutions will remain where they are now: as minor characters and spectators. Once we sideline Captain Cook it will be easier to deal with other and lesser intruders. As long as we rely mainly on written documents, and as long as Europeans, Americans, and similar others are seen to dominate our pasts as main actors or manipulators of local people to carry out their designs, our histories will remain imperial histories and narratives of passive submission to transformations, victimisations, and fatal impacts. There have been tragic and awful victimisations. But from a long-term perspective, which is the best kind of historical outlook, what is of more importance is how people, ordinary people, the forgotten people of history, have coped and are coping with their harsh realities, their resistance and struggles to be themselves and hold together. Patricia Grace's brilliant novel, *Cousins* (1992), is the best record I have yet read of how an ordinary Oceanian family struggles to maintain its coherence in the face of adversity. Until relatively recently, Pacific histories have generally been silent on resistance and the struggles to cohere that went on, mostly unnoticed, through decades of domination and exploitation. Even in the late 1960s, Hawai'i and New Zealand were still touted as societies of multiracial harmony.

In order to bring to centre stage grassroots resistance and other unnoticed but important events for our peoples, we must refocus our historical reconstructions on them and their doings. The new knowledge and insights we might gain from this reversal of historical roles could open up new and exciting vistas. Let others do their reconstructions of our pasts; we have dialogue with them, we form alliances with some. But we must have histories—our roots and identities—that are our own distinctive creations.

After we look at the people, we introduce into our historical reconstructions the notion of ecological time, which is perhaps both the egg and the chicken to a marked emphasis in our traditional notions of past, present, and future. Our modern conception of time stresses linear progression in which the past is behind us, receding ever further, while the future is ahead, in the direction of our progression, which is an evolutionary process leading to ever higher and more advanced forms. Let it be clear that by "linear progression" I include the notion of cumulative development or modernisation, which is equated with progress towards the capitalist utopia, the dream of the wretched of the earth. Lineality was not absent in our traditional notions. In fact it was particularly strong in Central and East Oceania,[2] where it featured in genealogies, especially those of high chiefs and their deeds. Histories obtained from genealogies have a lineal emphasis, and they are also aristocratic histories. In West Oceania, where genealogies were relatively shallow, lineality was expressed in other ways. Oceanian lineality, however, was neither evolutionary nor teleological, but sequential; it had much to do with assertions of rights for succession and inheritance, not, perhaps ever, with evolutionary development as we know it.

We can see our traditional nonlinear emphasis in the languages of Austronesian-speaking peoples, which locate the past in front and ahead of us and the future behind, following after us. In her remarkable book *Native Land and Foreign Desires,* Lilikalā Kame'eleihiwa says:

> It is interesting to note that in Hawaiian, the past is referred to as *Ka wa mamua,* "the time in front or before." Whereas the future, when thought of at all, is *Ka wa mahope,* or "the time which comes after or behind." It is as if the Hawaiian stands firmly in the present, with his back to the future, and his eyes fixed upon the past, seeking historical answers for present-day dilemmas. Such an orientation is to the Hawaiian an eminently practical one, for the future is always unknown, whereas the past is rich in glory and knowledge. It also bestows upon us a natural propensity for the study of history. [1992, 22–23]

In the Fijian and Tongan languages, the terms for past are *gauna i liu* and *kuonga mu'a,* respectively—*gauna* and *kuonga* meaning "time" or "age" or "era," and *liu* and *mu'a* meaning "front" or "ahead." When Fijian and Tongan preachers or orators point their fingers to the past, they never say *gauna i liu* or *kuonga mu'a* and point to the back; they say the appropriate term and point ahead. The conception of the past as ahead or in front of us is not a mere linguistic construction. It has an actual historical basis in the documentation of our oral narratives on our landscapes. I shall say more on this later.

The terms *liu* and *mu'a* may be used as verbs—as in *au sa liu* and *teu mu'omu'a,* meaning "I am going ahead of you," or more graphically in the popular Fiji English, "I am taking the lead," which is the literal translation of *au sa liu.* The past then is going ahead of us, leading into the future, which is behind us. Is this, then, the case of the dog chasing its tail? I believe so. From this perspective we can see the notion of time as being circular. This notion fits perfectly with the regular cycles of natural occurrences that punctuated important activities, particularly those of a productive and ritual/religious nature that consumed most of the expended human energy in the Oceanian past and still do in many parts of our region today. This is ecological time, an idea that we could use for the reconstruction of many of our histories. I shall return to this point shortly. But let me say here that the English language incorporates this notion of past as "ahead" and future as "behind," as in "let us pay tribute to those who have gone before us," and "the generations that are coming behind us."[3] But the main emphasis in the Western and hence our modern notion of time is not circular, except in Christian calendrical rituals and festivals, but rather linear, progressive, and teleological, which might have been strengthened immeasurably by the rapid changes that have occurred since the industrial revolution.

That the past is ahead, in front of us, is a conception of time that helps us retain our memories and be aware of its presence. What is behind us cannot be seen and is liable to be forgotten readily. What is ahead of us cannot be forgotten so readily or ignored, for it is in front of our minds' eyes, always reminding us of its presence. Since the past is alive in us, the dead are alive—we are our history.

Where time is circular, it does not exist independently of the natural surroundings and society. It is very important for our historical reconstructions to know that the Oceanian emphasis on circular time is tied to the regularity of seasons marked by natural phenomena such as cyclical appearances of certain flowers, birds, and marine creatures, shedding of certain leaves, phases of the moon, changes in prevailing winds, and weather patterns, which themselves mark the commencement of and set the course for cycles of human activity such as those related to agriculture, terrestrial and marine foraging, trade and exchange, and voyaging, all with their associated rituals, ceremonies, and festivities. This is a universal phenomenon stressed variously by different cultures. With its unquenchable thirst for growth propelled by its mighty technologies, however, modern society is disengaging itself from natural cycles, which, as we shall see, is the major factor driving global environmental degradation.

Time is so subsumed under these cycles and other more discrete events that precise dating, which is a main preoccupation of mainline history, is of no importance. In the past, as it is with many people today, it was not so much *when* events occurred but rather *where, how,* and in what *sequences* they occurred that was important. Of course our ancestors did not have the means to date events. This, however, should not unduly concern us, especially when we are dealing with remote pasts. Moreover, when things occur or are done in cycles, dating, which is tied to lineality, is in fact not quite relevant. Now that we have the means for dating we use them; but in our reconstructions, it is broad periods and the social and political implications for the present of remembered pasts that are paramount.

Of equal importance in the consideration of the relationship between Oceanian societies and nature is the role of technology. The driving force that propelled human activities was the knowledge and skills developed over centuries, fine tuned to synchronise actions with the regularities in nature. As it provided the vital link between society and nature, technology cannot be dissociated from either. It was a vital and compatible component of the cycles. This made for balance and continuity in the ecological relationship. "Living in harmony with nature" is a more popular way of putting it. For a genuinely Oceanian historiography, we could use this notion to reconstruct some of our pasts in terms of people's endeavours always to adapt and localise external borrowings and impositions, fitting them to their familiar cycles. In this way they actively transformed themselves rather than just being passively remodelled by others.[4] This has been the case since the early settlement of Oceania; it still holds true for much of our region today. Anthropologists, especially those who worked in the Papua New Guinea highlands in the 1950s and 1960s, have in fact recorded such indigenisations among peoples who had just encountered westerners for the first time. And more recently, growing numbers of anthropologists are writing their works as historical anthropology and historians are writing theirs as ethnographic histories.[5]

But things have not always fitted into familiar cycles, which creates a problem that lies at the core of the study of social change and history. One of the cardinal tenets of modernisation, a notion of linear progression that takes little or no consideration of natural cycles, is the necessity and hence the moral imperative of the *transfer of technology.* Modern technology, conceived of as independent of both nature and culture, can therefore be transferred anywhere in the world unencumbered with natural or cultural baggage. This notion has, on application, wreaked havoc on human lives and nature everywhere. The attempt to transfer high technology as the engine for modernisation to societies that have for ages accommodated themselves to natural cycles of ecological relationships is like leading an elephant into a china shop.

But, it may be asked, what is the relevance of this view of history to the linear processes that presently dominate modern society, worldwide processes driven by transnational capital and the global economy? We have other means of dealing with this kind of situation and must use them. We should, however, keep in mind that we live in societies with most of our peoples dwelling in rural and outer-island communities. Much of their existence involves their endeavours to cope with invasive technologies and adapt them to their familiar cycles. Most of us who are urbanised and living in accordance with the demands of the contemporary global culture still maintain relationships with our nonurban relatives and are therefore entangled in the tussle between tradition and modernity, however defined. Their narratives are therefore ours, as has always been the case before modernisation separated us. For the reconstruction and analysis of historical processes of this kind, we could use the notion of the spiral, which connotes both cyclic and lineal movements.

Most of our remote and so much of our recent pasts are not documented and therefore lie outside the purview of mainline history. We must in that case devise other methods, based on different perspectives of history, to reconstruct such pasts to suit our purposes, including those of maintaining the depths of our roots and strengthening our autonomous identities. We have to bequeath to future generations more memories of our recent past and our present than we ourselves remember of our remote pasts. We must remember and reconstruct as much of our pasts as we can to present to the future.

This is not sentimental nonsense on the part of someone who is getting on in years and reflecting on lost youth and idealised pasts; far from it. Recall Milan Kundera's immortal statement: "The struggle of man against power is the struggle of memory against forgetting." Relationships of power such as those between nations, classes, and other groupings are often characterised by the dominant going out of their way to erase or suppress memories, or histories, and implant what they wish in order to consolidate their control. Take, for example, the history of England and the British Empire taught in colonial schools, in place of local histories, so as to direct human thought and therefore more easily manipulate the colonised. The near extinction of Celtic languages in the British Isles, and the suppression of New Zealand Maori and Hawaiian languages, were deliberately engineered to destroy memories and cultures and thereby absorb the vanquished more smoothly into the dominant cultures. Fortunately this has not been completely successful. A major feature of the Maori and Hawaiian struggles for sovereignty is the revival of their indigenous languages and histories.

Other examples may also be taken from Central and East Oceania where our aristocracies have for centuries encapsulated most if not all our remembered pasts. Most of our ancient and even our more recent oral histories are about the lives and heroic and horrific deeds of our great chiefs, their families, and kin groups. Our histories, cultures, and group identities are focused almost entirely on them. Without them we have only a few roots, because the lives and deeds of the majority of our peoples have been erased from memory. This is a pillar of the aristocratic power over us. We cherish and respect our connections to our aristocracies, mainly because we have no choice; and for the same reason "we love and respect our oppression," as a waggish colleague puts it. Nevertheless, they are the major component of our heritage and so we must carry them all, the good and the ugly, for only then can we learn properly from our histories.

In view of this, we have to take careful note of our indoctrination by our contemporary elite groups and ruling classes—of which we, the senior staff of the university, are members. How and for what purposes are we directing our people's thinking and memories? What do we allow to be taught thoroughly, to be taught only cursorily, or not taught at all, in our schools and other institutions of learning? What do we read or not read, hear or not hear, see or not see in our mass media? Where and wherefore are the silences?

I am reminded here of a piece of advice by Machiavelli to his Prince. It was rather extreme, so I do not advocate its being followed to the letter. Machiavelli said that when you kill someone, kill everyone else connected to him so that no one survives to nurse the memory and plot to do you in.

We cannot therefore have our memories erased, foreshortened, or directed. With weak roots we would be easily uprooted, transplanted, grafted upon, trimmed, and transformed in any way that the global market requires. With little or no memory, we stand alone as individuals with no points of reference except to our dismally portrayed present, to our increasingly marketised national institutions, to international development agencies, international lending organisations, transnational corporations, fit only to be globalised and whateverised, and slotted in our proper places on the Human Development Index. Let Eric Waddell have the final say on this:

> I hear the same voices in the Pacific today: "It is forbidden to speak Fijian (Hindi, Cook Island Maori, Samoan, Tongan . . .) in the classroom and the school playground." Everything must take place in English (or French). On entering the school the child must take leave of his past, his present, his kin. The classrooms and corridors may be decked with flowers, the teachers smiling, the joys immense. But it is like a door which is sealed behind him, so that a new world may be designed afresh, unhindered by the weight of tradition, unmoved by the voices of the ancestors. And in this new world, . . . each child stands alone: small, remote and ultimately helpless. [1993, 28–29]

I submit that this is not confined to our primary schools. It is characteristic of all our formal educational institutions and our workplaces. In our educational programmes we provide our students with materials that for the most part have been produced by people in the United States, Britain, and other leading countries of the global system. Ideas that we impart to our students pertain mainly to these societies, even though they may be projected as universal verities. We and our students digest these notions and then enter international discourses on progress almost always on other people's terms. We play their games by their rules, and accept the outcomes as inevitable and even morally desirable, although these may be, as they have often turned out to be, against our collective well-being. We are thus eroding whatever is caring and generous in our existence, sacrificing human lives and our natural surroundings in order to be competitive in the world market. We need therefore to be much more inventive and creative than we have been, for our own humane development. Our vast region has its own long histories, its storehouses of knowledge, skills, ideals for social relationships, and oceanic problems and potentials that are quite different from those of large landmasses, in which hegemonic views and agendas are hatched.

In addition, we could use the notion of natural cycles and our traditional ecological relationships to formulate our own philosophies and ideologies for resistance against the misapplication of modern technologies on our societies. We cannot do away with the global system, but we can control aspects of its encroachment and take opportunities when we see them in order to create space for ourselves. We could, for example, formulate a benign philosophy that would help us pay greater reverence and respect to our natural environment than we do today. I have touched on the development of traditional technologies to link natural cycles and cycles of human activity in enduring, total ecological relationships. As has been pointed out, one of our major contemporary problems is that linear progression is based on systematic and cumulatively destructive deployment of dissociated technology on dissociated nature and society, as required by the global economy. But if we believe that we are dependent on nature to tell us, as it told our ancestors, when and how to derive our livelihood from it, and how to care for it, we would think very hard before meddling with it for short-term advantage, knowing that our actions could break the cycles and probably cause irreparable damage to ourselves. Earlier I said something about the idea of the spiral as a model for historical reconstruction. We could go further and incorporate this notion in the formulation of an Oceanian ecological ideology, tying linear development to natural cycles, with the view of guiding the applications of modern technologies on our environment. Our long-term survival within Oceania may very well depend on some such guidance. Kalani Ohele, a Hawaiian activist, told me something that has been said before but is worth repeating here: "We do not own the land, we only look after it."

This leads us to the consideration of the relationship between history and our natural landscapes. I first came upon this theme in reading 'Okusitino Māhina's thesis, although I later found out that this has been done for Hawai'i and that the New Zealand Maori have been working on it for quite some time. Most of our sources of history are our oral narratives inscribed on our landscapes. All our important traditions pinpoint particular named spots as landing places of original ancestors or spots from which they emerged, as arenas of great and decisive battles, as sites of past settlements, burials, shrines, and temples, as routes that important migratory movements followed, as markers of more localised mobility out of one's own into other people's territories, which made much of the land throughout our islands enduringly contested by parties deploying not only arms but also oral narratives, including genealogies, to validate their claims and counterclaims. Populations seem always to be in flux and so too were the dispositions of land, providing much of the flexibility and motion to the operation of Oceanian societies. All of this is recorded in narratives inscribed on the landscape. Our natural landscapes, then, are maps of movements, pauses, and more movements.

Sea routes were mapped on chants. Nearly thirty years ago, Futa Helu wrote a series of articles on a particular dance chant, the *me'etu'upaki,* believed to be Tonga's most ancient. The chant is in an archaic form of the language that almost no one today understands, which is taken to be the indication of its antiquity. Helu's translation reveals that it is about a voyage from Kiribati to Tonga. The verses of this chant pinpoint places along the route arranged precisely in their geographic locational sequence.[6] I believe that the chant is the chart of a long and important sea route that people used in the past. I once asked a very knowledgeable seaman how people of old knew sea-lanes, especially between distant places. He replied that these were recorded in chants that identified sequences of landfalls between points of departure and final destinations. Distances were measured in how long it generally took to traverse them. I believe that the Australian Aborigines did roughly the same with their songlines that connected places all across their continent from coast to coast.

Our landscapes and seascapes are thus cultural as well as physical. We cannot read our histories without knowing how to read our landscapes (and seascapes). When we realise this, we should be able to understand why our languages locate the past as ahead or in front of us. It is right there on our landscapes in front of our very eyes. How often, while travelling through unfamiliar surroundings, have we had the experience of someone in the company telling us of the associations of particular spots or other features of the landscape traversed with past events. We turn our heads this way and that, and right ahead in front of our eyes we see and hear the past being reproduced through running commentaries. And when we go through our own surroundings, as we do every day, familiar features of our landscapes keep reminding us that the past is alive. They often inspire in us a sense of reverence and awe, not to mention fear and revulsion.

These are reasons why it is essential not to destroy our landmarks, for with their removal very important parts of our memories, our histories, will be erased. It may be significant in this regard that in several Austronesian languages the word for "placenta" and "womb" is also the word for "land." Among a group of people once well known to me, the Mekeo of Papua New Guinea, the dead were traditionally buried in front of their houses on the sacred ceremonial ground that ran through the centre of their rectangular villages. The term for the ceremonial ground is *ango inaenga,* the "womb of the land." The womb nurtures and protects the unborn child, as the land nurtures and provides security for humanity. At the end, the departed are returned to the womb of the land. From the womb we come and to the womb we return. It is a much richer and more ennobling image than "earth to earth, ashes to ashes," in which there rings an inglorious destiny for our mortal remains.

This very intimate association between history and the natural landscape and between us and our Earth is, I believe, the basis for the oft asserted and maligned notion that we are spiritually and mystically related to the lands to which we belong. It is very difficult for the urban-born and the frequently mobile to comprehend this kind of relationship. They have little or no appreciation of the fact that for very many of us, people and land are indivisible. Indigenous Fijians have always insisted that the word *vanua* means the land and its people. The Tongan terms for traditions and culture are *tala e fonua* and *ulungaanga fakafonua,* the "stories of the land" and "the way of the land," respectively. People are one with their culture and land. This brings to mind an occasion in the late 1960s when a Tongan extended family was brought to Fiji and resettled on native land in western Viti Levu. It transpired that when the last surviving member of a particular "landowning" lineage passed away, the clan to which the lineage belonged searched for nonresident offshoots and located the only ones in Tonga. These latter were invited to come to the land, awaiting its rightful complements. They belonged to it and vice versa, they went to it, and they are still there today. No one else could have occupied it in the accepted manner. When I bought a house in Suva a few years ago, my colleagues who were from outside Oceania or descendants of more recent arrivals commented on it as an act of property investment. But indigenous Fijian and Tongan colleagues and friends said, without exception, "so you are going to live here forever," or words to that effect. To some I was acquiring a property, disposable at a good profit at some future date; any improvement I might make on it would enhance its sales value. To others I was establishing a home that would tie me to it forever; any improvement on it would be a further contribution for the benefit of my family and future generations. In saying that I was going to live here forever, my friends meant not just me but also my descendants.

There is a vast difference here that shows diametrically opposed perceptions of our relationship with our world: world as property versus world as lasting home—home as a heritage, a shrine for those who have cared for it and passed it on to us, their descendants. For those of us who hold this view, our relationship with our Earth is indeed spiritual.

Opponents and even some sympathisers of resistance and sovereignty movements in Oceania and elsewhere frequently express utter contempt for assertions of this kind of relationship, the importance of which is felt most acutely when your ancestral homelands are gone or threatened. I recall having read a statement by a New Zealander who characterised Maori spirituality as so much mumbo jumbo. This could have been an expression born of ignorance, or an unconscious trivialisation of something that is powerfully threatening. I once met a very liberal-minded person in Australia who talked of Aboriginal spirituality in a manner that was perfectly correct and no more. At least she was trying to come to grips with it. Whatever others may say, we need to include in our philosophy of reverence for nature a strong element of spirituality that we may borrow from our pasts or other people's pasts, or even invent for ourselves, because our Earth is being subjected to intolerable pressures.

To remove a people from their ancestral, natural surroundings or vice versa—or to destroy their lands with mining, deforestation, bombing, large-scale industrial and urban developments, and the like—is to sever them not only from their traditional sources of livelihood but also, and much more importantly, from their ancestry, their history, their identity, and their ultimate claim for the legitimacy of their existence. It is the destruction of age-old rhythms of cyclical dramas that lock together familiar time, motion, and space.

Such acts are therefore sacrilegious and of the same order of enormity as the complete destruction of all of a nation's libraries, archives, museums, monuments, historic buildings, and all its books and other such documents. James Miller (1985), the Australian Aboriginal educator best known for his book *Koori,* told me that his people, the Wonnarua, who once occupied the Hunter Valley all the way down to the central coast of New South Wales, have a history that dates back only to the beginning of the British settlement. Their lands are gone, and only a handful of the words of their original language are still in use. They have no oral narratives, no memory whatsoever of their past before the invasion and obliteration of their ancestral world.

We, who are more fortunate, cannot afford to believe that our histories began only with imperialism or that as peoples and cultures we are the creations of colonialism and Christianity. We cannot afford to have no reference points in our ancient pasts—to have as memories or histories only those imposed on us by our erstwhile colonisers and the present international system that seems bent on globalising us completely by eradicating our cultural memory and diversity, our sense of community, our commitment to our ancestry and progeny, and individualising, standardising, and homogenising our lives, so as to render our world completely open for the unfettered movement of capital and technology. We must therefore actively reconstruct our histories, rewrite our geography, create our own realities, and disseminate these through our educational institutions and our societies at large. This is absolutely necessary if we are to strengthen our position for surviving reasonably as autonomous peoples within the new international order.

We, who are more fortunate, cannot afford to let our own compradors continue to conspire with transnational corporations and others to strip and poison our lands, our forests, our reefs, our ocean. Many of the critical problems that we confront today are consequences of acts, such as large-scale land deals, committed by our very own ancestors. We must be careful not to continue repeating similar acts, thus bequeathing to future generations a heritage of misery. We cannot talk about our spiritual relationship with Earth while allowing ourselves and others to gut and strip it bare.

We need to strengthen cultures of resistance within our region. For generations, our peasantries have resisted many if not most introduced "development projects" simply through noncooperation or through withdrawal of support as soon as they realised the harmful implications of such projects for their lives. In more remote eras our ancestors devised very effective and at times drastic methods of political resistance. For instance, the greatest fear of high chiefs in the past was the ever-present threat of assassination. The heads of despots everywhere in Oceania were taken regularly, in a literal and figurative sense. The Tu'i Tonga, for example, were so often taken care of that they created a lower paramountcy to be a buffer between them and an oppressed and enraged population. Series of assassinations of these officials compelled them to establish an even lower paramountcy to take the heat. And so it went. And so we must follow and resist the erosions, the despoliations, and the exploitations that are going on in our region. We owe this much to ourselves and to the future.

I conclude with the following reflection on past, present, and future. Wherever I am at any given moment, there is comfort in the knowledge stored at the back of my mind that somewhere in Oceania is a piece of earth to which I belong. In the turbulence of life, it is my anchor. No one can take it away from me. I may never return to it, not even as mortal remains, but it will always be homeland. We all have or should have homelands: family, community, national homelands. And to deny human beings the sense of homeland is to deny them a deep spot on Earth to anchor their roots. Most East Oceanians have Havaiki, a shared ancestral homeland that exists hazily in primordial memory. Every so often in the hills of Suva, when moon and red wine play tricks on my aging mind, I scan the horizon beyond Laucala Bay, the Rewa Plain, and the reefs by Nukulau Island, for Vaihi, Havaiki, homeland. It is there, far into the past ahead, leading on to other memories, other realities, other homelands.

Notes

This essay, first published in Borofsky (2000), evolved from talks delivered as an Oceania Lecture at the University of the South Pacific, October 1994, and at the Pacific Writers Forum, East-West Center, August 1994. The cosponsors of the Pacific Writers Forum, the Program for Cultural Studies, East-West Center, and the Center for Pacific Island Studies, University of Hawai'i, provided large amounts of uninterrupted time to think and write early drafts of this essay. I benefited greatly from discussions with Sudesh Mishra, Nora Vagi Brash, Marjorie Crocombe, and Alberto Gomez outside Lincoln Hall. Vilsoni Hereniko, Geoff White, and Vimal Dissanayake were wonderful organisers, hosts, and stimulating company. Haunani-Kay Trask and Lilikalā Kame'eleihiwa of the Center for Hawaiian Studies encouraged me to continue writing this essay. Tony Hooper read the original version and gave much-needed constructive comments. I am indebted to them all.

1. See, for example, *Contemporary Pacific,* vol. 1, nos. 1 and 2, 1989; vol. 3, no. 1, 1991.

2. In order to do away with the racial/cultural connotations of the threefold division of Oceania into Melanesia, Micronesia, and Polynesia, I have regrouped the region geographically as follows: West Oceania (the islands of New Guinea, Solomon Islands, Vanuatu, New Caledonia); North Oceania (Belau, the Marianas, Guam, Federated States of Micronesia, Marshall Islands); Central Oceania (Nauru, Kiribati, Tuvalu, Uvea [Wallis] and Futuna, Fiji, Tonga, Tokelau, Samoa, American Samoa, Niue); East Oceania (Cook Islands, French Polynesia, Pitcairn Island, Rapanui, Hawai'i, Aotearoa New Zealand). Central Oceania is the region of the greatest overlapping and mingling of populations and cultures.

3. Tony Hooper alerted me to this point as well as to Oceanian lineality.

4. At a time when I was fairly despondent about developments in our region, Marshall Sahlins converted me to this view through personal conversations and in a University of the South Pacific 25th Anniversary Lecture he delivered in Suva in early 1993. He has since published this lecture as "Goodbye to *Tristes Tropes:* Ethnography in the Context of Modern World History" (1993). This is essential reading for all of us who are concerned with the construction of our pasts, with our cultures, and with our future prospects.

5. See the articles by historians and anthropologists in Brij V. Lal (1992), Donald H. Rubinstein (1992), and Robert Borofsky (1994). For an excellent piece of historical ethnography see Geoffrey White (1991). Beautifully written, in accessible language, it is about Santa Isabel in the Solomon Islands.

6. See Futa Helu (1979, 1980). At the December 1994 conference "Pacific History: Deconstructing the Island Group," at the Australian National University, it was pointed out that voyagers from Central Oceania travelled to Kiribati and even as far as Pohnpei.

References

Borofsky, Robert, ed. 1994. *Assessing Cultural Anthropology.* New York: McGraw-Hill

———. 2000. *Remembrance of Pacific Pasts: An Invitation to Remake History.* Honolulu: University of Hawai'i Press.

Davis, Tom. 1992. *Island Boy: An Autobiography.* Suva: Institute of Pacific Studies, University of the South Pacific.

Grace, Patricia. 1992. *Cousins.* Auckland: Penguin.

Hau'ofa, Epeli. 1993. "Our Sea of Islands." In *A New Oceania: Rediscovering Our Sea of Islands,* edited by Eric Waddell, Vijay Naidu, and Epeli Hau'ofa. Suva: School of Social and Economic Development, University of the South Pacific. Reprinted in *Contemporary Pacific* 6 (1) (1994):148–161.

Helu, Futa. 1979 and 1980. "Tongan Poetry IV: Dance Poetry." *Faikava* (Nuku'alofa) 4:28–31 and 5:27–31.

Kame'eleihiwa, Lilikalā. 1992. *Native Land and Foreign Desires.* Honolulu: Bishop Museum Press.

Lal, Brij V., ed. 1992. *Pacific Islands History: Journeys and Transformations.* Canberra: Journal of Pacific History, Australian National University.

Māhina, 'Okusitino. 1992. "The Tongan Traditional History *Tala-ē-Fonua:* A Vernacular Ecology-Centred Historico-Cultural Concept." PhD thesis, Australian National University, Canberra.

Miller, James. 1985. *Koori: A Will to Win. The Heroic Resistance, Survival, and Triumph of Black Australia.* North Ryde, NSW: Angus & Robertson.

Rubinstein, David H., ed. 1992. *Pacific History.* Guam: University of Guam Press and Micronesian Area Research Center.

Sahlins, Marshall. 1993. "Goodbye to *Tristes Tropes:* Ethnography in the Context of Modern World History." *Journal of Modern History* 65:1–25. Reprinted in *Assessing Cultural Anthropology,* edited by Robert Borofsky. New York: McGraw Hill, 1994.

Trask, Haunani-Kay. 1991. "Natives and Anthropologists: The Colonial Struggle." *Contemporary Pacific* 3 (1) (Spring):159–167.

Waddell, Eric. 1993. "The Power of Positive Thinking." In *A New Oceania: Rediscovering Our Sea of Islands,* edited by Eric Waddell, Vijay Naidu, and Epeli Hau'ofa. Suva: School of Social and Economic Development, University of the South Pacific.

White, Geoffrey. 1991. *Identity Through History: Living Stories in a Solomon Islands Society.* Cambridge: Cambridge University Press.

Our Place Within

Foundations for a Creative Oceania

As in other places in our world, modern institutions in Oceania, such as the University of the South Pacific (USP), are continually being restructured and otherwise redesigned to synchronise their activities with the processes of globalisation. In this fiercely competitive environment there should be no room for free-ranging imagination and creativity of the kinds not tailored to the demands of the global economy.

But such a space exists within the University of the South Pacific, our region's leading training institution for globalisation. And it is part of my purpose here to talk about its genesis, its objectives and hopes for the future, and the actual steps taken over the nearly seven years of its existence in contributing to the nurturing of a creative Oceania. More important, the narrative shows what can happen when particular sets of ideas are acted upon. It is these notions, and their potential for generating actions leading to desired ends, that underlie the narrative about the development of the particular space mentioned above. Discussions of these ideas, and experiments with their implementation, could help us to refine and invent continuously better ways of effecting changes that enhance our capacity for creativity and the attainment of cultural autonomy.

The development at our university of a space or community dedicated to reflection, exploration, and originality is based on the belief that in order to be continuously creative, we must have spaces where we give free rein to our imagination and ample time to experiment with and develop new forms and styles, new movements, sounds, and voices, that are unmistakably ours. The arts community that we are nurturing is infused with the sense of continuity with our pasts, which we plumb for inspiration and guidance. History and culture may no longer be priority subjects and disciplines in our schools and institutions of higher learning, but living pasts and the sense of historical and cultural continuity are essential components of our societies. They define us and provide the bases from which we venture into other worlds. The people of the island of Tanna in Vanuatu conceive of their universe in terms of the tree and the canoe. The tree symbolises rootedness in culture, while the canoe stands for movements along sea routes that connect people of different island locations. The canoe is history—the working out of relationships established through travel and movement of materials from one island to another. One may extend this metaphor to include present-day connections between Oceania and the surrounding continental landmasses and cultures. One may even say that since it is made of wood, the canoe is part of the tree, and its potentials are to a large extent determined by the qualities of the tree from which it was made. History and culture are thus enmeshed.

It is therefore essential for us in Oceania that the creative arts and other forms of cultural production take up what our formal educational institutions have marginalised as nonessential in the world of the twenty-first century. For us they are necessary tools for the attainment and maintenance of autonomy within a homogenising global system. Our social, economic, and political institutions are woven into the larger world system; any free space within will have to be established through creative cultural production. And this is what the present and rising generations of Oceania's growing and widely dispersed intelligentsia are furiously involved in today. From their far-flung bases in Guam, California, Hawai'i, Cook Islands, New Zealand, Fiji, Samoa, Tonga, Solomon Islands, Papua New Guinea, Australia, and increasingly elsewhere within and beyond the Pacific Basin, they are connecting through the Internet and face-to-face encounters to discuss and work towards a culturally creative and free Oceania.

What is happening in the cultural arena of our university should be seen in this context. In 1992 the USP Council decided that a programme on Pacific arts and culture, modelled on the Polynesian Cultural Center (PCC) in Hawai'i, be established at the university's Suva campus. The Polynesian Cultural Center is Hawai'i's major tourism attraction. For several decades now, thousands of Pacific Islands students at the Mormon Church's Brigham Young University in Hawai'i have performed at the PCC, contributing to its phenomenal success while incidentally paying for their fees and lodging.

The USP, which by design had largely ignored Pacific cultures as a field worthy of serious teaching and research, was unexpectedly confronted with an instruction to take on art and culture as a way of conserving identity and enabling poor students to perform for tourists for their tuition and other expenses. As normally done in such a situation, the USP formed a committee to look into the matter. The committee unanimously rejected the idea of our becoming involved in tourism as entertainers. That was the only thing it was united upon.

It should be noted here that Fiji was then going through a period of upheaval following the racist military coups of 1987 and the subsequent installation of an exclusive indigenous Fijian regime and a racist constitution. As a result, anything to do with Pacific cultures was intensely disliked by the so-called progressive elements within the university. This was reflected in the deliberations of the committee. A vocal group comprising expatriates and Oceanians of internationalist convictions viewed traditional cultures as barriers to the progress of liberal democracy and respect for human rights. They opted for doing away with Pacific arts and cultures entirely and replacing them with an enlightened, broad-based expressive arts programme to be offered to our degree and diploma students.

There was one dissenting voice that insisted on a programme in the creative arts of contemporary Oceania. He argued that because of the virtual absence in our university region of our own contemporary visual and performing arts, what we needed most urgently was to encourage their emergence and development. Without this, any teaching of the arts would take us away from our cultures into those of the West, aborting any chance for the development of our own contemporary forms. It would hasten our complete absorption by other cultures. It should also be noted here that although traditional arts and cultures were sponsored widely in the USP region, much of it in the interest of tourism and the hospitality industry, not one institution sponsored the development of our own contemporary arts. There are modern artists working in Fiji, for example, but most are either foreigners or Oceanians who have studied fine arts overseas or learned from resident Western artists. The content and some of the materials used may be local, but the styles, the perspectives, and the aesthetic values are all non-Oceanian.

Because of the fundamental disagreement within the committee—and the committee's departure from the council's decision that the programme be on Pacific arts and culture—nothing was done for several years until the council reminded the university of its unimplemented decision. One day I was informed of my appointment to head a new committee whose membership was to be selected by the chairperson. Things started to move quickly from then. All those who held contrary views in the previous committee were uninvited. Membership was all Oceanian academics who were themselves writers, poets, and the university's lone visual arts lecturer. And since none of us had any experience in establishing and managing a general arts programme, the committee invited the very experienced Ulli and Georgina Beier, who were then directing a third-world arts centre at the University of Bayreuth, Germany, to visit us, look into our situation, and write a report that would help us. A most valuable report was eventually presented to the university—pregnant with ideas and suggestions but with no concrete recommendations for a systematic course of action.

All the good ideas contained in the report, as well as those of the committee members, were simply floating in the air. This was the situation when the decision was made that a new section of the university, to be called the Oceania Centre for Arts and Culture, would be launched in early 1997 and I was assigned to do the job. That was all there was to it. There were no directives, no set programmes to be implemented. All other sections of the university were meticulously planned, structured, and vetted thoroughly before they were approved and launched and staff were recruited to implement already laid out programmes. Not the Oceania Centre. It was pushed through committees very quickly, perhaps because it was an unexpected conception that could not be aborted. Had it been still-born no one would have noticed except the director, who would then be on the streets looking for another job.

As the director I was provided with a programme assistant, a part-time cleaner, a very modest budget, and a small architecturally nondescript building, partly hidden under huge trees, located significantly on the boundary between the main part of the university and the residential quarters for staff and students. We were thus placed on the margins, where we have since blessedly remained.

There was no formal launching of the centre, which simply came into being on 1 February 1997, when I, the programme assistant Lillian Thaggard, and the part-time cleaner Mili Naikece moved into our assigned premises—and found ourselves left well alone to do as we liked. This was something that we never dreamt of, and we took the opportunity to establish as much freedom as possible acting as we saw fit. It gave us the chance to actually try out, in complete freedom, the things that we had dreamt about over the years, never thinking that we would one day be given the unique opportunity that had just befallen us. It was a trust that we did our best to be worthy of. Six years down the line, we still enjoy complete freedom, though still with modest budgets, marginality, limited space, and bare-boned staffing. And we developed the cardinal rule of not making insistent demands on the university, especially on its financial resources. Such demands would attract unwelcome attention to what we were not supposed to be doing. Complaints would have attracted a similar response, so we never complained.

The freedom also allowed us ample time to develop ideas about aims, objectives, and programmes to be pursued without being unduly stressed by pressure to meet deadlines. There were no deadlines. But we were cognisant of the expectation that sooner or later we would have to produce tangible results.

Thus, while thinking about our objectives, etc., we embarked on our first project—the creation of a home for the arts—by transforming our existing premises and surroundings into a space that was conducive to creativity, an environment that people would find relaxing and welcoming. Most buildings at the university are coldly functional. Available funds enabled only limited extension to the existing building by the addition of areas with floors and roofs but no walls. The relatively small size and openness of the space obliges people to work closely with and in sight of each other. It also means that those who walk and drive by can see what is happening: dancers, painters, sculptors, and musicians all working and performing in the same space. And because of the absence of a proper gallery or auditorium, all the centre's exhibitions and most performances are held in the same open space, for everyone to view, free of charge. Even labourers mowing and sweeping the university grounds, the kind of people who would not normally enter enclosed galleries and auditoriums, feel comfortable enough to come and see our artists work or rehearse or to view our exhibitions. People can see both the processes of creation and the final outcome in the same space. It is very important in building a public for the arts that the process of creation is open to viewing. What we have actually developed is not only a home for the arts but also a space that reflects an important aspect of community life in Oceania: noisy openness with very little privacy. And as in real, relatively small communities, there is much sharing, with everyone influencing and learning something from everyone else, and occasionally getting on each other's nerves. Painters, sculptors, dancers, and musicians interact with and help each other—a process that seems to be leading towards the natural growth of a kind of integrated arts phenomenon, something that is much talked about but difficult to realise. A few years ago while on a visit to New

Zealand, I went to the opening of a school for creative and performing arts. Everything was contained in one large building, and as one passed through it one was weighed down by the silence that pervaded the soundproofed, air-conditioned edifice. All activities were held behind closed doors. One heard music or viewed rehearsals or performances only when one opened the appropriate doors. There were very good reasons for that kind of spatial arrangement, but I was still impressed by the stark contrast with the centre that we had built.

While constructing our home for the arts, we were able to produce our aims and objectives and, as well, the programmes that would lead towards our goals. Our first objective was, and still is, the cultivation of a spirit of creative originality that would lead to the flourishing of contemporary visual and performing arts that are firmly rooted in our histories, traditions, and adaptations to the changing international environment that is affecting every facet of our existence. This creative process will remain focussed on experiments and originality, which are necessary if we are to take our cultures out of the mire of imitation and cloning reproduction. What is generally taken for creativity in our region is largely the adoption, and occasionally refinement, of things generated mainly outside Oceania or the unceasing reproduction of the original creations of our forebears in ages past.

Second, the creativity unleashed should reflect important principles of our societies—in particular reciprocity, cooperation, openness to community, and transmission of knowledge and skills through observation and hands-on experience. In the modern world art is considered an individual's affair. We, however, view art from the interest of a collective and encourage our artists to nurture each other. We do not spurn individualism; we choose to give priority to the collective. Some people say that, considering our financial situation, we should weed out the less gifted artists. But in order to sustain the collective spirit we carry everyone, until members decide for themselves that they stay or leave. In Oceanian communities, for example, dance and music are a matter of communitywide participation. Everyone joins in, either performing or supporting. But we know who are the best, the good, and the weak. The weak are generally put in back rows, where they are not too conspicuous, or assigned supporting roles. The idea is that everyone has a part to play.

Third, we aim to develop our own criteria for assessing the aesthetic merit and other cultural values of our contemporary creations. We must be satisfied with what we are doing, according to our own standards, before we present them. In the formal teaching sections of the university, each department has an external adviser, usually an internationally renowned scholar from overseas, who regularly assesses the departmental offerings to make sure that they measure up to internationally accepted standards. These standards are always set elsewhere—namely in the West. We still look to outsiders for approval, a lasting legacy of our colonial past.[1] But we at the Oceania Centre are convinced that on matters of cultural creativity, which express who and what we are, we must be self-assessed by our own standards of evaluation.

For this we go back to what remains of the creations from our pasts. The arts of our ancestors grace the great museums, galleries, and private collections of Europe, the Americas, Australasia, and Japan. They are works of power and beauty, as impressive as their creators' navigational and other historic achievements. Contemplation of these works, together with our contemporary creations and our traditional sense of aesthetics, could help us to produce for the first time written sets of standards that are our own. It is significant that this concern with our own aesthetic values has risen simultaneously with our university-based intellectuals' rising interest in Oceanian epistemologies, philosophies, and values. Pursuing our own value systems does not mean that we cut ourselves off from the rest of the world. I have written elsewhere that "we learn from the great and wonderful products of human imagination and ingenuity the world over, but the cultural achievements of our own histories will be our most important models, points of reference, and sources of inspiration. This should help to bring out the best in us, while we remain true to ourselves."

Fourth, we aim to produce visual and performing arts that are regional, transcending our national insularity and cultural diversity. To date, when people talk or write of Oceanian art they refer to the creations of different countries or cultural groupings within a particular geographic region known as Oceania. The focus is necessarily on diversity. Our centre is called Oceania deliberately to signify its regional nature and aspirations. We aim to produce for the first time contemporary arts that all of us in Oceania would consider ours and would be recognised by others as such. This is putting into practice what I have been advocating over the last decade: a regional Oceanian identity based on our common inheritance of a large swathe of the Pacific Ocean.

The development of new art forms that are truly Oceanian is very important in another respect. It allows our creative minds to draw on far larger pools of cultural traits than those of our tiny individual national lagoons. It makes us less insular without being submerged in the amorphousness of the global cultural morass. As the largest of our multicultural regional institutions, our university is an ideal location for focussed developments in regionalism. The centre's emphasis on Oceanian forms and identity in artistic and cultural production should contribute significantly to regional cooperation and unity in our part of the world.

Fifth, we aim to harness creativity to our practical struggle for survival. In Oceania all forms of creativity were integral to the daily and ceremonial life of the community; there was no such thing as art for its own sake. In the world today, the best way for the Oceania Centre to do this is to tie the arts to the most urgent need for protecting our oceanic environment: the sea and the islands. This should enable us to remain true to the tenets of our communities and to contribute significantly to the most important global environmental agenda: the protection of the ozone layer, the forests, and the oceans, for the continuity of life on earth.

Sixth, we aim to produce a corpus of contemporary works readily accessible to our educational institutions and our communities. Most of the creations from past eras have been either destroyed or removed to museums and private collections far from Oceania. Very few of us can access them directly. As an alternative, we can see them as photographs in art books so expensive that they might as well have been kept in the basement of the British Museum.

Our centre is often compared with the very generously endowed Jean-Marie Tjibaou Centre in New Caledonia, which is building up an impressive collection of contemporary Pacific arts from all over Oceania. Representatives of the Tjibaou Centre are able to travel outside New Caledonia and buy expensive works for their collection. They are also able to bring the best artists in the region to Noumea to exhibit their works, some of which the Tjibaou Centre buys. The Oceania Centre, by contrast, cannot afford to buy works of art from anywhere. One of the most recent of John Pule's canvases, for example, could wipe out half the centre's annual budget. We are nevertheless building up a growing collection, virtually all of them works done by our own trainees and established artists, who have grouped themselves into an association, the Red Wave Collective. Virtually all of what we have collected are works that were created at the centre. We collect for posterity, keeping in mind the loss to powerful countries in the past, as today, of the best that we have produced: our people and other irreplacable treasures.

Finally, we believe that it is in the field of creative cultural production that we are most likely to produce the best that we are capable of—rivalling or even equalling original creativity anywhere. People who visit our centre are often surprised by our trainee artists' show of remarkable talent, their natural creativity, enthusiasm, and so forth. Very recently a New Zealand-based Samoan conductor and composer of serious music was invited to start a university choir to rehearse and perform his works, the lyrics of which are in Pacific languages. Two hundred students volunteered and, within a week of evening rehearsals of what was completely new to them, gave an impressively smooth performance at our graduation ceremony to an awe-struck audience that had rarely seen a choir of that magnitude before. The maestro said that it normally takes him six weeks of rehearsals in Auckland to produce the same result.

This goes to show that within our own domain we can readily excel. In academic fields of natural and social sciences, information technology, and so forth, our students are generally confronted with enormous difficulties because the origins of these disciplines are alien to our societies, compelling our students to learn and perform by other people's unfamiliar rules and regulations. Within our own domain, however, we set rules that, because of their emergence from our circumstances, we can readily accommodate and be comfortable with, enabling us to perform at our very best and at our own pace. This does not mean that we cannot perform successfully in other people's fields, far from it. But there we do not usually perform with the same degree of confidence, inventiveness, verve, and enjoyment. In Oceanian societies, we prefer to do things with enjoyment, mixing work and pleasure shamelessly. Globalisation, on the other hand, is such a serious, mechanical, joyless, and soulless enterprise that the flames in people's spirit are often extinguished at the outset, making it very difficult to rekindle them. Much time and effort are thereby consumed wastefully.

In short, the actual realisation of the talents of our creative minds should enable us to carve out an ample space within the global system to allow us to breathe freely—a space in which we have control over what we do, and where to go, to be ourselves; a space recognised as ours, in which visitors abide by our rules as we abide by theirs when we enter their territories; a welcoming space from which we could reach out to others with the naturalness, assurance, and civility that normally come from those who are at ease and at peace with themselves and with their surroundings.

The financial and other material resources provided by the university have helped to shape the centre's programmes as well as its progress towards attaining its ambitious goals. We believe that setting our sights high will propel us to do much more than otherwise.

From the beginning our modest budgets prevented us from becoming just another formal teaching institution, leaving us free to move into other and new directions, away from the dominant preoccupation with globalisation. Teaching arts as part of the university's degree and diploma programmes would have entangled us and buried us under the far larger and more powerful teaching schools. I insisted from the beginning that we must be a freestanding unit. As a former head of the USP's largest teaching school, spending inordinate amounts of time trying to cajole and pacify contrary and independent-minded academics, I found that moving to establish a one-person unit where I try to reason only with myself was such a relief that my gout vanished forever.

That's by the way. In any case, formal teaching would have entailed recruiting staff from abroad, most probably from Australia and New Zealand. Courses would have been developed to conform to "international standards" with textbooks based on Western art history, aesthetic perceptions, and such. And like the rest of the university, we would have developed away from our Oceanian base. In their consultancy report, "Cultural Identity in Oceania," Ulli and Georgina Beier wrote of the negative effects of art schools in colonial India and Africa where the British "introduced the European method of learning and seeing. Anatomy, perspective, life drawing and heavy emphasis on European art history from the renaissance to the end of the nineteenth century. Students with strong personalities and original creative talents often took years to liberate themselves. They had to go back to rediscover their traditional wall paintings, their ancient calligraphy or folk art in order to overcome the process of alienation they had been subjected to." We are not necessarily opposed to the teaching of arts as such. We believe that at this stage of our development we should focus on producing contemporary works that will eventually become resources for teaching and research in our region. When we are ready to teach, we will not be so dependent on non-Oceanian resources as we are today.

Formal teaching of the arts would have denied access to our programmes to the largest body of the most creative original talents in our societies. These people are school dropouts or leavers who do not qualify to enrol in university programmes. Most of our trainee visual and performing artists are from the ranks of the unemployed, part-timers, and casuals. Thus instead of teaching we facilitate. We provide a space, materials, and mentoring to any would-be artist who needs these to develop his or her talent. Aspiring painters, sculptors, musicians, and dancers come to the centre, where they are imbued with the idea of developing our own distinctively Oceanian arts.

Most university students are not interested in the arts; they have enrolled in the university in order to become bureaucrats, managers, professionals, and business entrepreneurs. Regional governments do not provide scholarships for the creative arts. Only those from wealthy and well-connected backgrounds can afford to enrol in arts schools overseas as private students. Most of the rest have to redirect their energies into nonartistic activities, or join the ranks of the unemployed or casually employed.

Very early on it became clear that to develop contemporary Oceanian arts the centre would rely on the full-time artists that it nurtures. We could not rely on established artists; they are set in their ways and are not amenable to redirection. That is to be expected. We therefore offered workshops for beginners to which we invited, through newspaper advertisements, young people between eighteen and twenty-four years of age, who are not on full-time study or employment, because these latter would treat art as a hobby to be indulged in their spare time. For our first painting workshop, at the beginning of 1998, we selected the New Zealand-based Niuean artist, John Pule, to conduct. Pule was chosen because his works at the time were inspired by Oceanian tapa and mat designs, and he worked in the earth colours used by weavers, tapa painters, specialists in traditional lashings, and such. Of painters with Pacific Island origins, Pule was the most distinctively Oceanian in his creations. Artists who have emerged from that workshop became mentors to newcomers to the centre. None of our artists has had any formal training except what little they obtained at school. Since they are such newcomers with no experience in the arts, they take readily to the centre's goals and are inspired by them. On two occasions we had workshops on techniques, conducted by an Australian and a South African, respectively. Our trainees were directed to paint scenery and realistic human forms, which they enthusiastically did. But as soon as the workshops were completed they returned of their own volition to what they now called contemporary Oceanian styles but each time greatly enriched by their brief experience in the closest they have come to formal training.

Our contemporary dance programme was started by a mature university student who had some choreographic experience in traditional Polynesian dance. Allan Alo first came to the centre to participate in a painting workshop, but he expressed his wish to develop his choreographic talent. The centre provided him with a series of short-term appointments as artist in residence to develop expertise in contemporary Oceanian dance that weaves together strands of dance movements from across the region as well as from modern Western and Eastern dances. Since becoming our full-time choreographer he has established the Oceania Dance Theatre, which has staged performances of contemporary Pacific dance not previously seen anywhere in the university region.

In 1998 the centre appointed as artist in residence a young and talented musician, Sailasa Tora, who had come to me to declare his intention to revolutionise Fijian music. Since he was obviously out of his mind, he was most welcome to the loony bin. His compositions have influenced the development of a new Fijian music inspired by ancient chants.

Workshop and artist in residence programmes have enabled the Oceania Centre to provide a modicum of training to our visual and performing artists. These help to set them on their journeys of discovery. The rest depends on the individual artist's innate talent and drive, mutually supported by members of the arts community that we have built together.

Since the beginning we have worked only with the resources allocated to us by the university, most of which come from funds triennially provided by our governments and some from the New Zealand and Australian governments. We have never gone directly to outside sources for funds. We believe that on matters concerning our cultures and identity, we must rely on ourselves and not on anyone else. In the process of our development we have discovered that we actually have a great deal more resources available in our environments and in ourselves than we have been led to believe. The problem with our dependency today is not so much the lack of resources but the judicious and creative use of what is available and the will to live within our means and develop from there. I have often been told to go to funding agencies for what we need. They said that there is so much money out there to be tapped! We have resisted that—finding it exciting and challenging to produce as much as we can from what appears to be so little. It is the best way for attaining and maintaining real autonomy. The community that we have started building cannot really be ours otherwise.

The freedom that we have obtained for the centre in relation to the university as a whole is that which we allow our artists. We never tell them what to do or not to do as artists. They work at their own pace, and they come and go as they wish. We are there to support them, guide them when needed, and help them to grow as artists. We always advise our artists to think of what does not exist and bring it to life. This may be the fairest explanation for what we, as a community, have been able to do with what we have had at our disposal over the relatively short period of our existence. Seeing such things happen, and contributing in some ways to their creation, makes one profoundly appreciative of what it means to be free in an increasingly managed and controlled world.

So far we have been working quietly at the centre and have not bothered to use the Internet to publicise what we are doing. We do not have a website. We have not even produced a single brochure. We prefer to focus on building our strengths first before we step outside. But after nearly seven years, we feel that we are in a position to expand into other parts of our region. In the near future we hope to establish our programme in Honiara with the Solomons creative artists that we have nurtured at the centre. In the long run we foresee expansion into the rest of the university region using our extension centres and campuses as bases of operation. Beyond that we would like to visit places outside Oceania proper, to share and exchange with the inhabitants thereof.

In 1996, while trying to produce a thematic concept that would "give the Oceania Centre a clear, distinctive, and unifying identify," I wrote the following: "The theme for the centre and for us to pursue is the ocean and, as well, the interactions between us and the sea that have shaped and are shaping so much of our cultures. We begin with what we have in common and draw inspiration from the diverse patterns that have emerged from the successes and failures in our adaptation to the influences of the sea. From there we can range beyond the tenth horizon, secure in the knowledge of the home base to which we will always return for replenishment and revision of the purposes and directions of our journeys. We shall visit our people who have gone to the lands of diaspora and tell them that we have built something: a new home for all of us. And taking a cue from the ocean's ever-flowing and encircling nature, we will travel far and wide to connect with oceanic and maritime peoples elsewhere, and swap stories of voyages we have taken and those yet to be embarked on. We will show them what we have created; we will learn from them different kinds of music, dance, art, ceremonies, and other forms of cultural production. We may even together make new sounds, new rhythms, new choreographies, and new songs and verses about how wonderful and terrible the sea is, and how we cannot live without it. We will talk about the good things the oceans have bestowed on us, the damaging things we have done to them, and how we must together try to heal their wounds and protect them forever." We still hold on to these sentiments. They belong to the constellations that we use to guide us on our journey towards an ever creative and free Oceania.

Notes

This essay was originally delivered as the 2003 Forge Memorial Lecture, Australian National University, Canberra, on 8 October 2003.

1. In Australia, I believe, that cultural cringe has only fairly recently been outgrown.

PART III

Creating

OVERLEAF: *On the Reef,* Frederick Butafa, 2000

The Writer as an Outsider

IT IS SAID THAT, at the age of forty, most middle-class men have led, for at least fifteen years, a secure, sedentary life. By then they have raised their families, reached the pinnacle of their achievements, and gained the respect of their fellow Establishmentarians. Having attained all or most of what they have aspired to, or reached the highest point to which they can ascend, they are confronted at forty with the imminence of their declining years, the stark outlines of their mortality. This often leads such men to resort to desperate measures to retain their powers, to maintain the illusion of youthfulness and vigour. Sometimes such steps can be pathetic, sometimes comical, and occasionally tragic.

Five years ago, on reaching forty, I began for the first time to shed my prolonged adolescent ways and embark on doing what I should have done some fifteen or twenty years earlier. I began to settle down into a cosy, middle-class existence. I had by then been in the Tongan civil service for just over two years. The job was a middle-level posting but sufficiently high and prestigious for me to be admitted into the elite cocktail party circles, where I rubbed shoulders with the movers of the land and their foreign advisers. I had built a comfortable house surrounded by a five-foot fence to mark off my territorial domain from those of my near-destitute neighbours, most of whom were my relatives. I had raised two dogs, a couple of pussycats, and a few chickens, which flew over the fence into other people's cooking pots. I had a family with two children, the kind of family size one could maintain comfortably without forgoing a typical bourgeois existence.

As one of the two resident natives with PhD degrees, I found my views and opinions on a wide range of issues much sought after by local residents as well as by an endless stream of visiting experts, advisers, academics, postgraduate students, journalists, some ordinary tourists, and even a few international crooks and wheeler-dealers. It did not seem to matter to others that my views and opinions on most matters were decidedly ill informed; I dished them out freely, learning along the way to live with my shortcomings since everyone around seemed to have at least as many shortcomings as I if not more. In any case, what I had to offer did no harm to anyone; neither did it do much good. Several times a year I was invited overseas to offer my views at conferences, seminars, or workshops or to be a consultant to such international agencies as the Asian Development Bank and the World Bank. These were lucrative assignments supposedly in the service of the poor.

Things seemed to be working out fine at the time. I was moving towards a comfortable position in the Tongan Establishment. I had an undemanding job, a comfortable home life, a degree of respectability, and a growing reputation at home and in certain circles abroad. I also had the right amount of ill repute to add spice to an otherwise humdrum existence. What else could a man want in life? But during this period of settling in, something else was happening. My new mode of life went against every habit that I had acquired over the previous forty years, during which I had always been an outsider to every society I had lived in. In none of these had I lived sufficiently long to identify completely with it or to be accepted totally by it. By the age of nine, for example, I had lived in three different Papua New Guinea societies, in Australia, in Fiji, and in Tonga. Later I moved residence to Fiji, then to Australia, Canada, the West Indies, Papua New Guinea once more, then back to Australia, Tonga, and most recently to Fiji for the third time. Such a rootless background is decidedly not conducive to permanent membership in any national establishment.

Since much of my mobility was as a schoolboy and later as a university student on scholarship (up to as late as my mid-thirties) I had, by the age of forty, never been in any position of power or even closely associated with people in leadership positions. My experience with prefects and bullies in boarding schools created in me a lasting distaste for power. From about the age of eleven, I had associated closely only with underdogs—real ones as well as privileged underdogs such as university students. Socially I could really be comfortable only in the company of powerless people. Thus my induction into the Establishment of power wielders was completely at variance with my background.

Essentially, like most people without power, I view the elite with a large measure of scepticism. This scepticism is bolstered by a knack for detecting absurdity in situations. I believe that the two are closely associated, perhaps as inseparable as two fingers. As far as I can remember, I have always delighted in absurdity in others as well as in myself. This may be a function of powerlessness in society. Different people react differently to the circumstances of their lives; for myself, I tend not to believe in what I see; most serious things somehow appear ludicrous and I usually dismiss them with a laugh. But the laughter is not always light; it often is very seriously mocking. This sensitivity to absurdity is a natural development from my early fantasies—as a teenager I often dreamt about being a comic actor; I wanted to make people laugh. At boarding schools in Tonga and Fiji I spent an inordinate amount of time telling outrageous stories, the earthier the better. I did not like old wives' tales from grandmothers; I delighted in tall tales and dirty stories composed on the spot by randy adolescents. I was also a natural clown, something that was never appreciated by my schoolteachers. In my final year of school in Fiji I played Mr. Hardcastle in Oliver Goldsmith's *She Stoops to Conquer,* a role which affected me so much that for weeks afterwards I went about like a doddering old man and was pronounced dotty by my schoolmates.

I also developed a lasting fascination with cartoonists and comedians, my favourites being comedians Charlie Chaplin, Buster Keaton, the Three Stooges, Laurel and Hardy, and Lenny Bruce and cartoonists Rigby, Oliphant, Cooke, Leunig, and Walt Kelly. I liked reading Swift, Cervantes, Voltaire, Chekhov, Evelyn Waugh, G. V. Desani, early V. S. Naipaul, Sholom Aleichem, Giovanni Guareschi, Chester Himes, Mike Royko, Russell Baker, Art Buchwald, and the cartoonists and writers of *Punch.* The relevant point, however, is that anyone who delights in absurdity and considers himself a clown can never be a serious candidate for permanent membership in any Establishment, especially in the postcolonial South Pacific where the elites take themselves so seriously that they have not developed a thick skin. A reviewer of my recent book says "now that his unseemly irreverence has been noticed he will never work for officialdom again." He is probably correct.

One final detail is relevant to this brief autobiographical account. I had a strong religious background, being raised in an evangelical Christian missionary family. I first grew up at a mission station in Papua New Guinea and spent nine years in two mission boarding schools. I shall not go into detail on this matter; suffice it to say that anyone who is familiar with Christian evangelical and fundamentalist groups knows how heavy and stifling the atmosphere can be. I moved away from organised religion in my mid-twenties and by the time of my entry into the Tongan Establishment I was already a confirmed agnostic. In much of the South Pacific today, one's standing in a community depends to a large extent on one's professed religious faith and participation in activities sponsored by organised religion. Much of the social life of a community revolves around religious activities, and community services of numerous kinds are still, to a large extent, provided by religious organisations. A person who cuts his bonds with organised religion severs many of his ties with the community. An agnostic cannot, therefore, attain a good standing, for his beliefs place him outside the community.

My background of rootlessness, of being a perpetual outsider, a professional underdog, a clown at heart, a connoisseur of absurdity, and an unbeliever, rendered me completely ill suited to the life of sedentary respectability that a national Establishment provides and even demands. So while I was settling into the Tongan Establishment, a small persistent voice kept saying, "What are you doing where you don't belong?" I tried to ignore it but could not. The same question could also have been asked of me by most other members of the Establishment. My being new, my seemingly anti-Establishment record, my still unconventional ways—all marked me out as an oddity. Strangeness cuts both ways.

One day, while I had little or nothing to do in my office—and this was certainly not unusual—I wrote "Home at Last," a little verse of hardly any aesthetic merit that nevertheless distills my experiences over a period of five years.

HOME AT LAST

I am tired
of being naive
talking to myself
winding handless clocks
and bailing the ocean
tomorrow
I shall go
to church, the police station
parliament house, the courts
other corridors and the market
places
they say
where you can buy truth easily.

This verse was not deliberately devised; it just somehow came out—perhaps it was the devil who did it. Tongan preachers, who generally condemn vagrancy and laziness, are fond of saying that for those who have nothing to do, the devil finds bad deeds. That may or may not be—it's neither here nor there—but the fact is that "Home at Last" says something about the two phases of my life in Tonga. In the first phase, which lasted three years, I operated outside the Establishment, first as a University of the South Pacific research fellow and later as a dropout, a failed poet. It was a period of frantic creativity; I wrote three books and a few poems; I started writing my satirical stories and was publishing a literary magazine.

Throughout these three years I also assumed the role of social critic, a self-appointed prophet crying in the wilderness, or more correctly a self-righteous public gadfly detested or ignored by the powers that be. Up to that point, no well-educated Tongan commoner had taken on the role of public critic of the Establishment. I got away with it because I was protected by the prestige of a PhD degree and because I used for my arguments examples from the local culture and history as well as verses from the Bible. But it was still something new to the society, and I was isolated. There was no group of like-minded people to whom I could go for support or comfort. Eventually, I got tired of my loneliness. Hence the first part of "Home at Last." The other part of the poem relates to the second phase of my life in Tonga. I had sold out. The saying "If you can't beat them, join them" aptly describes that situation.

Having pondered the contents of "Home at Last" and their implications, I realised that my days in the Establishment were numbered. (I had done a similar thing once before. In early 1975 I read to the ANZAAS conference in Canberra a paper that was a strong indictment of anthropology in the South Pacific. At the end of the session, a friend told me, "You are biting the hand that feeds you." What he did not know was that in writing the paper I realised that I would not remain in the mainstream of professional social anthropology. And it was the "outsider" in me that was at work again in this instance.) I must make it clear that I was not at the time harbouring strong sentiments against the Establishment. For those who are in it, it provides a comfortable and enjoyable existence. The elite accepted me, admittedly with strong reservations, but they knew that given time I would eventually be absorbed totally. They have a saying that a stray sheep will always in the end get back to the fold. Putting it in the words of an old Tongan proverb, "A dog will always return to its vomit."

My two years in the civil service taught me respect for humility. I think that to be a good civil servant one has to be a very dedicated person with a strong sense of discipline so that one can control one's personal predilections for the good of the organisation. I am too individualistic and lacking in the kind of discipline needed to be a good organisation man. When I left the service I was cleansed of my former prejudices against bureaucrats. So while I wrote (and will continue to write) satirical things about them, I could not do so with personal venom. The same holds true for other targets of my writing. I cannot shoot them; my intention is to send all of them happily to paradise with an overdose of cocaine.

It took me two more years to extricate myself from my comfortable but alien existence. When the time came I packed my bags and my family and moved out of Tonga altogether to the more familiar, insecure existence at the University of the South Pacific Laucala Campus, which has the knack for gathering into its bosom the most outrageously weird academics to be found anywhere between Chile and Indonesia.

What I have so far revealed about myself is very selective; there are numerous things I have dreamt and thought about, things I have done or left undone, and things I am likely to do or are likely to be done unto me, that I have no intention whatsoever of revealing to anyone. I take consolation in the knowledge that everyone else does exactly the same, save those who are sufficiently insane to consult psychiatrists or to confess to their priests. But still, the account is relevant to me as a writer. I have written very little in fact, and the little that I have written has had no impact on anyone or anything. But I am one of the small but growing number of Pacific Islanders whose publications have attracted some notice within and without the region. So, being one of the few, I have been easily qualified as a member of that tiny elite group that is supposed to be contributing to the emergence of a new literature in our region. I am most happy to be a member of this group since it does not exist. What does exist are individual writers, poets, and scholars who work mainly by themselves (often because of their being isolated in their own islands) and occasionally meet each other as friends or enemies. Membership in this nebulous group is sufficient for one to be invited to conferences abroad, to be consulted on cultural matters in the islands, and to be sent forms to be filled out for storage in the CIA computer centre somewhere in Honolulu.

I am reminded here of the fact that in the late 1960s and the 1970s any Pacific Islander with a PhD or even an MA in anything could literally become whatever he wished to be, or he could become what he had never imagined becoming. In the name of localisation and regionalisation, greatness was liberally showered on unsuspecting persons by the promoters of native peoples. It had some weird effects on these peoples' attitudes and consequently on the lives of those around them. For instance, after I completed my doctoral programme I returned to Tonga to find myself an Expert on more things than I care to enumerate. I had no formal training whatever in demography or environmental studies, but shortly after my arrival I was asked to contribute a paper on the effects of rapid population growth on environment and society. Based largely on common sense and a good deal of guesswork, it was capped with predictions of dire consequences should people dare ignore what I said. That ten-or-so-page paper was miraculously transformed into a forty-page mini-picture book that instantly established me as an Expert on population problems and environment. Since the publication of *Our Crowded Islands* I have spent so much time and ingenuity trying to avoid being exposed as a fraud that I have willy-nilly become a real imposter. I sincerely recommend that anyone who is mediocre or worse but wants to become great and famous should immediately do away with his or her obscure life and be reborn as a native South Sea Islander or, alternatively, join the ranks of the academic or administrative staff of the University of the South Pacific, where it is impossible to go wrong unless you have brains or sense.

Having acknowledged my insignificance as a writer, and my other shortcomings, I return to the problem of autobiography and its relevance to a very minor author. I shall largely focus on myself as a dweller of the outer spaces of society. My book *Mekeo,* which is a structural functionalist piece of ethnography, reflects an aspect of the writer as outsider. A major theme of the book is the structural opposition between the outside and the inside, with a tabooed peripheral no-man's land demarcating the two realms. I took a whole society, with its physical environment, its social, symbolic, and cosmological systems, and analysed it in terms of the structural relationships between inside and outside: the inner and outer spaces through which people and powers move endlessly in their endeavour ultimately to reconcile the irreconcilable. But my bias shows up for I concluded and still believe that the sources of extraordinary power, knowledge, creativity, and freedom are located outside the boundaries of conventional society and, moreover, that heaven above is the domain not of a benign father figure but of the horned Mephistopheles to whom the soul of humanity has been sold since the beginning of time. My sympathy with underdogs is evident in my analysis of the relationships between elder and younger brothers, between seniority and juniority. I found that though institutional powers were held through ascription by elder brothers, younger siblings often went outside to bring new and often greater powers, which they used to subvert the prescribed order and so eventually impose their dominance. I do not know how much of what I wrote of the Mekeo was a projection of my own personality, including my personal sympathies. It does not really matter. For I believe that every analysis of social and cultural situations is in part a self-exploration by the analyst.

As a discipline anthropology is the classic example of the "outsider." It developed as a study of other cultures and has, with some minor changes, remained so even today. Although I entered the discipline by accident, I was eventually attracted to it perhaps because it was a case of courtship between birds of the same feather. I studied other people, I wrote about them, I liked most of them, but I could never become one of them. This is true of all anthropologists. However much we understand and like the people of the cultures we study, we always remain outside their charmed circles.

As one remains outside, one is exposed to the elements that can chill the soul and heighten the sense of isolation as one looks into a house where the hearth glows, the beds are soft, and the laughter peals are infectious. I often long to enter, to belong to the community in which I live at any particular time; but only in Tonga, for reasons of ancestry, and forced and voluntary identification, could I come close to belonging, as I have described here. But I could not, and the internal conflict was often painful. "In Transit," the last poem I wrote, brings this out clearly and poses the question of who is the real native.

In Transit

(thoughts from the windows of the Palace Office)

Grey light filters
Through dusted leaf screen
Thrilling laughter from Pangai
Tossed by the beat of breakers
On coral walls
That check an ocean

To make it crawl
To alien guns guarding
The fishermen's beach
Another day has gone
Passed in time-filling chats
And floorboard creaks
In this old house
That nurses fading portraits
Of those who led our land
Stood awhile
With the Norfolk pines
Evergreen sentinels
Dwarfing the red spires
Of the kauri chapel
With arched doors
And arched windows
Foreign structure
That has sat
Six generations
Breathing briny weathers
Marking Kava Calls
To become almost Tongan
As you and I
Only much older and
With the alien pines and guns
Will still remain
To gauge the tide when
After brief sojourn
In our native land
We leave.

Shortly after writing "In Transit" I applied for a job that removed me from the civil service and set me on the road that eventually led me out of Tonga.

As an outsider observing events taking place in island societies, I tended to regret what I considered to be harmful changes in people's lives. I felt this regret most strongly in Tonga because there I was both an outsider and an insider. "Our Fathers Bent the Winds" expresses this regret vividly.

Our Fathers Bent the Winds

Only yesterday
the Sands of Sopu brightened the shores of Nuku'alofa,
horse-drawn carts crawled half-awake the green roads,
and we sent men and money to Missions abroad.
Our fathers bent the winds and strode the waves
to bring the Kula and Mothers of Kings from Upolu,
fine mats from Manu'a and the royal studs of Lakemba for the Forbidden
Daughters.
And did not Maui Kisikisi pierce the horizon with his javelin?
Or the Suppressor-of-Waves speed slabs from Uvea
for the terraced tombs of the God-Kings?
But the Sands of Sopu are gone,
broken beer bottles strew the Sacred Shore,
the tennis court from Salt Lake City marks the grave
of Sālote's lawn,
and the one-time nation of givers,
dreaded jaws of the ocean,
begs for crumbs from the Eagle and the Lion.
Yesterday Tangaloa made men,
But the God of Love breeds children.

Although this poem may be viewed as an idealisation of the past, I have resorted to such allusions in order to highlight our contemporary situation in the islands. To me the most unfortunate things that colonialism, Christianity, and international capitalism have given to the Pacific Islands have been, first, the transformation of hitherto self-sufficient, proudly independent people into wards of rich and powerful countries; and, second, as a consequence of forced dependence, the compulsion on people to compromise their integrity and use all manner of trickery in order to survive in an economic and political world over which they have no meaningful control. Without a certain degree of control over one's life and destiny, one loses the most essential parts of one's being: self-esteem and the respect of others. I first came across evidence of this in 1960 among the Aborigines in the outskirts of an Australian country town. I have recently noticed it in some sections of urban communities in the islands. Among island elites, on the other hand, the necessary compromise of integrity in order to secure foreign aid has wounded many souls. It makes people bitter and ultimately turns them cynical.

Finally, being an outsider has enabled me to maintain a degree of detachment so that I can observe life more clinically than I could otherwise. This measure of detachment is partly responsible for my tendency to see, behind the seriousness with which we conduct our daily lives, the hollowness and futility of many of our efforts and aspirations. This view of life may be jaundiced, but it informs much of what I have written recently.

All the things that render me unsuitable for life in the Establishment—together with my experiences as a researcher and fraudulent expert and my impotent rage at what is happening in the islands today—have together contributed much to what I have written, especially so with the *Tales of the Tikongs*. Just about everything said in that book is based on personal experience and thus reveals something about myself. Throughout, however, I, like most Pacific Islanders, have maintained intact my sense of humour, and with it much of my remaining sanity.

I shall conclude this essay by saying something about my reasons for indulging in nonacademic writing. First, I write to entertain—to make people smile and laugh. We need to smile and laugh occasionally, especially in this age of macho-crazed, sabre-rattling presidencies and prime ministerships. I get much satisfaction when a reader says that he has enjoyed my tales and that he chortled and laughed as he read. I get even greater satisfaction when readers tell me that they appreciate the social criticism that underlies the humour.

The second reason for writing fiction is the freedom and the enjoyment it has afforded the writer. I wrote my first tale after I had just completed revising my anthropological thesis for publication and had embarked on writing a very dry account of a research project that had occupied me for nearly two years. Those were arduous and almost soul-destroying exercises. Writing my first story was such a refreshing experience that I decided to change tack completely. In academic writing I always felt hampered. I chafed under the strict rules of verification and the requirement to be well versed in the ever-changing, ever-disappearing paradigms and models of explanation, faddish and remote from the realities of existence. I bristled against the obligation to read the unreadable, and to pay homage to intellectual ancestors, contemporary masters, and immediate superiors, if one were to survive in the fiercely competitive jungle. Most of all I was repelled by the jargon-laden obscurantism, the crassness, and the crudity of much of the social scientific literature. In nonacademic writing, on the other hand, I do not have to acknowledge any master past or present; I read only the works that I like; I set my own standards without reference to anyone else's; I invent and embellish freely, entertain, scold, and swear to my heart's content, provided only that what I write is internally consistent and intelligible. Fiction writing also affords me the freedom to play with words and meanings, something I relish enormously.

The third reason for writing nonacademically is that through it I am able to reach a much wider range of readership than I have been able to do with my other writings. It gives me pleasure to know that *Tales of the Tikongs* is a prescribed or recommended text for students of development studies, administrative studies, Pacific history, literature, and sociology; it is also read by the targets of my barbed comments and by those who would not be seen dead reading ethnographic or sociological tracts. I am most happy of all when I hear that my work is being read by my fellow Pacific Islanders.

But my main reason for writing is to develop a personal style that echoes the sounds of the spoken word in the islands. Like most Pacific Islanders, I was nurtured throughout my prepubescent years mainly on the spoken word. The written word is still strange to most islanders, even to those who are highly literate. To me, therefore, words are sounds with meanings. When I read, I do hear each word in my head rather than merely seeing and registering them. (That was why I failed disastrously when I joined a speed-reading class some twenty years ago; and I have remained to this day a very slow reader.) When I string words together on a piece of paper, what I actually do is to connect sounds, each of which should flow naturally and easily from the preceding sounds. I believe this is exactly the way that island masters of the spoken word use their language. The style that I have developed is an attempt to translate into writing the cadences of sounds as produced in the islands by storytellers, preachers, orators, people in supplication, people giving orders, arguing, quarrelling, gossiping, and so forth. All these sounds, these voices, can be heard in *Tales of the Tikongs.* The voice of the preacher/orator is stereophonically recorded in *Our Crowded Islands,* which not only is concerned with what is happening in some areas of life in the islands but, more important to me (when writing it), is an exercise in a particular style. When I read the paper to the conference, it had the intended effect. Marshall McLuhan is partly correct in saying that the medium is the message. Island preachers, orators, and other tellers of lies know it only too well. My writing, therefore, is not something only for quiet reading in bed or in a library. It is meant to be read aloud so that some of the beautiful and not so beautiful sounds of the voices of the Pacific may be heard and appreciated.

I have presented a very personal account because I was asked to by the organisers of this conference. I very rarely talk so personally about myself, least of all to total strangers. But I have perforce broken a long-established habit and hope that I have done an honest job of it. I also hope that I do not make a habit of it.

Note

This essay was originally a paper delivered at the conference "Self-representation in Literature," East-West Center, Honolulu, August 1984.

The Glorious Pacific Way

"I HEAR YOU'RE COLLECTING oral traditions. Good work. It's about time someone started recording and preserving them before they're lost for ever," said the nattily dressed Mr. Harold Minte in the slightly condescending though friendly tone of a born diplomat, which Mr. Minte actually was.

"Thank you, sir," Ole Pasifikiwei responded shyly. He was not given to shyness, except in the presence of foreigners, and on this sultry evening at a cocktail party held in the verdant gardens of the International Nightlight Hotel, Ole was particularly reticent.

Through the persistent prodding of an inner voice which he had attributed to that of his Maker, Ole had spent much of the spare time from his job as Chief Eradicator of Pests and Weeds collecting oral traditions, initially as a hobby but in time it had developed into a near obsession. He had begun by recording and compiling his own family genealogy and oral history, after which he expanded into those of other families in his village, then neighbouring settlements, and in seven years he had covered a fifth of his island country. He recorded with pens in exercise books, which he piled at a far corner of his house, hoping that one day he would have a machine for typing his material and some filing cabinets for their proper storage. But he had no money for these luxuries, so he kept to his exercise books, taking care of them as best as he could.

His work on oral traditions attracted the approving notice of the Ministry of Environment, Religion, Culture, and Youth (universally dubbed MERCY), a high official of which, who was also an intimate of Ole's, had invited him to the cocktail party to meet the diplomat visiting Tiko on a project identification and funding mission.

"Perhaps you could do with some financial assistance," Mr. Minte suggested.

"That'll help a lot, sir."

"We have money set aside for the promotion of culture preservation projects in the Pacific. Our aim is to preserve the Pacific Way. We want to help you."

"Very generous of you sir. When can I have some money?"

"After you've written me a letter asking for assistance."

"Do I have to? Can't you just send some?"

"Obviously you haven't dealt with us before."

"No, sir."

"Things are never quite that simple, you know. We have the money to distribute, but we can't give it away just like that. We want you to ask us first. Tell us what you want; we don't wish to tell you what you should do. My job is to go around informing people that we want to cooperate for their own good, and people should play their part and ask us for help. Do you get me?"

"Yes, sir. But suppose no one asks?"

"That's no problem. Once people know that they can get things from us for nothing, they will ask. And besides, we can always send someone to help them draw up requests. By the way, who's that jolly chap over there?"

"That's His Excellency the Imperial Governor."

"My God. I have something very important to tell him. I must see him now before he leaves. Come and see me tomorrow morning at ten at the MERCY building. Think of what I've said and we'll talk about it then. I'm pleased we've met. Good night."

Shortly afterwards Ole left for home, disturbed and feeling reduced. He had never before asked for anything from a total stranger. If Mr. Minte had money to give, as he said he did, why did he not just give it? Why should he, Ole, be required to beg for it? He remembered an incident from his childhood when a bigger boy offered him a mango then demanded that he fall on his knees and beg for it. Hatred for Mr. Minte surged in his stomach to be mixed with self-hatred for his own simplicity and for his reluctance to ask from a stranger while everyone else seemed to have been doing so without compunction. He needed a typewriter and some filing cabinets, not for himself but for the important work he had set out to do. Yet pride stood in the way. The Good Book says that pride is the curse of man. The Good Book also says, "Ask and it shall be given unto you." One should learn to ask for and accept things with grace. But he could not sleep well that night; his heart was torn—it was not easy to ask from a stranger if you weren't practised at it. He must do it nevertheless. There was no other way of acquiring the facilities he needed. Anyway, he supposed as he drifted into sleep, it's like committing sin: once you start it becomes progressively easier.

At ten the following morning Ole entered the MERCY office where Mr. Minte was waiting.

"Good morning, Ole. Have you made up your mind about seeking help from us?"

"Yes, sir. I'd like to have a typewriter and some filing cabinets. I'll write you a letter. Thank you."

"Now, Ole, I'm afraid that's not possible. As I said last night, things aren't so simple. We don't want to tell people what to do with the money we give, but there are things we cannot fund. Take your particular request for instance. My Minister has to report to our parliament on things people do with the money we give. Once politicians see that we've given a typewriter for culture preservation they will start asking embarrassing questions of my Minister. What's a civilised typewriter to do with native cultures? The Opposition will have a field day on that one. Most embarrassing. That won't do. . . ."

"But in my case it has everything to do . . ."

"You have to ask for something more directly relevant, I'm sorry. Relevance is the key that opens the world," Mr. Minte said, and paused to savour the profundity of his remark before turning on an appearance of astounding generosity.

"Look, we can give you $2,000 a year for the next five years to publish a monthly newsletter of your activities. Send us a copy of each issue, OK?"

"But I still need a typewriter to produce a newsletter."

"Try using a MERCY typewriter. You will have to form a committee, you know."

"A committee? What for? I've been working alone for seven years and no committee has been interested in me."

"Oh, they will, they will when good money's involved. The point, however, is that we don't give to individuals, only to organisations. You form a group, call it the Oral Traditions Committee or something, which will then write to us for assistance. Do you follow me?" Mr. Minte looked at his watch and lifted an eyebrow. "I'm sorry, I have to go now to talk with the National Women's Association. Don't you know that your women are more forthcoming and efficient than your men? When we tell them—sorry—suggest that they form a committee, they do so immediately. It's a great pleasure handling them. Their organisations have tons of money from us and other helpers. Think about it and come again tomorrow at the same time. See you then." Mr. Minte went out and disappeared into a black official limousine.

Ole remained in the office keeping very still, as was his habit when angry, breathing deeply until he had regained his equanimity. Then he rose and walked slowly to the office of his intimate, the high MERCY official, who sat quietly and listened until Ole had poured out his heart.

"The trouble with you is that you're too moralistic," Emi Bagarap said thoughtfully. "You're too proud, Ole."

"It's no longer a matter of pride, I've seen to that; it's self-respect."

"Self-respect is a luxury we can't afford; we have no choice but to shelve it for a while. When we're developed, then we will do something about dignity and self-respect. . . ."

"What if we are never developed?"

"We will develop! There's not a speck of doubt about that. You must cultivate the power of positive thinking," said Emi Bagarap looking wise, experienced, and positive.

"You must keep in mind, Ole, that we're playing international games in which the others have money and we don't. Simple as that. They set the rules and we play along trying to bend them for our benefit.

"Anyway, those on the other side aren't all that strict with their rules either. Take Mr. Minte, for instance. He offers to give you $2,000 a year for five years and all he wants is for you to form a committee and then the committee writes a letter asking for the funds and produces a newsletter regularly. But he didn't say anything about how the organisation is to be formed or run. See? You can get three or four friends and form a committee with you as chairman and treasurer and someone else as secretary. Get only those who're neither too interested nor too knowledgeable. That'll give you the freedom to do what needs to be done.

"Again, the letter asking for help will be from the Committee and not from you personally. Your self-respect will not be compromised, not that it really matters, mind you.

"Furthermore, Mr. Minte didn't say anything about the size of your newsletter, did he? Well. You can write it in a page or two taking about half an hour each month. And you don't have to write it in English either. And if you so wish you can produce two copies per issue, one for your records and one for Mr. Minte. I'm not suggesting that this is what you do; that would be dishonest, you see. I'm only pointing out one of the many possible moves in this game.

"Most importantly, Mr. Minte didn't say what you should do with the rest of the money. So. You pay, say, two dollars a year for your newsletter and with the balance you can buy a typewriter and four filing cabinets every year for five years.

"You see, Mr. Minte is very good and very generous; he's been playing international games for a long, long time and knows what's what. He wants you to have your typewriter and other things but won't say it. Go see him tomorrow and tell him that you'll do what he told you.

"But you must remember that in dealing with foreigners, never appear too smart; it's better that you look humble and half-primitive, especially while you're learning the ropes. And try to take off six stone. It's necessary that we're seen to be starved and needy. The reason why Tiko gets very little aid money is that our people are too fat and jolly. I wish the government would wake up and do something about it."

And so, Emi Bagarap, whose self-respect had been shelved for years, went on giving his friend, the novice, the benefit of his vast experience in the ways of the world.

When Ole left the office he was relieved and almost happy. He had begun to understand the complexities of life. Give me time, O Lord, he prayed as he headed towards the bus stop, and I'll be out there with the best of them.

"A word with you, old friend," Manu's voice checked him.

"Oh, hello Manu. Long time no see. Where've you been?"

"Watching you lately, old friend. You have that look on your face," Manu said simply.

"What look?" asked Ole in puzzlement.

"Of someone who's been convinced by the likes of Emi Bagarap. I'm worried about you. I know you and Emi have always been close, but allow me to tell you this before it's too late. Don't let him or anyone like him talk you into something you . . ."

"No one talks me into anything. I've never allowed anyone to do that," Ole cut in with visible irritation.

"You're already into it, old friend; it's written all over your face. Beware of Emi; he's sold his soul and will have you sell yours if you don't watch out."

"That's ridiculous. No one's sold his soul. We're only shelving certain things for a little while until we get what's good for the country."

"No, no, old friend. You're deceiving yourself. You're not shelving anything; you're set to sell your soul no less. Do it and you'll never get it back because you will not want to."

"You're wasting your time and mine, Manu. You belong to the past; it's time to wake up to the future," Ole snapped and strode away.

Next day when he met Mr. Minte he was all smiles. The smoothly seasoned diplomat raised an eyebrow and smiled back—he was familiar with this kind of transformation; it happened all the time; it was part of his job to make it happen.

"Well, Ole, when will you form the committee?"

"Tonight, sir."

"Congratulations, Mr. Chairman. Get your secretary to write me a letter and you'll get your first $2,000 in a month's time."

"Thank you very, very much, Mr. Minte; I'm most grateful."

"You're welcome. It's been a pleasure dealing with you, Ole. You have a big future ahead. If you need anything, anything at all, don't hesitate to contact me. You know, if we had more people like you around, the Pacific would develop so rapidly you wouldn't see it."

They shook hands, and as Ole opened the door Mr. Minte called out, "By the way, INESCA will soon hold a workshop in Manila on the proper methods of collecting oral traditions. It'll do you good if you attend. I'll let you know in a few weeks."

"Thank you again, Mr. Minte."

"Don't mention it. I'm always happy to be of assistance. Goodbye for now. I hope you'll soon get a typewriter and the filing cabinets."

Ole whistled his way home, much elated. That evening he formed the Committee for the Collection of Oral Traditions with himself as chairman and treasurer, his youngest brother as secretary, two friends as Committee members, and the district officer as patron. The Committee immediately set to work drafting a letter to Mr. Minte which was delivered by hand the following morning. Within a month Ole received a cheque for $2,000 and an invitation to attend a six-week training course in Manila. He went, leaving his house in the care of his elderly aunt, who did not understand what he was doing.

He found the course too confusing, but the throbbing nightlife of Manila more than compensated for its uselessness. He enjoyed himself so much that in the third week he received a shot of penicillin and some friendly counsel from an understanding physician.

On his return journey he bought a duty-free typewriter in Sydney, where he also ordered four filing cabinets to be shipped home. He was much pleased with his speedy progress: he had secured what had only recently been a dream. One day, he told himself as the aircraft approached the Tikomalu International Airport, he would take over the directorship of the Bureau for the Preservation of Traditional Culture and Essential Indigenous Personality. Both Sailosi Atiu and Eric Hobsworth-Smith were getting long in the tooth.

When he finally arrived home his aged aunt greeted him tearfully. "Ole, Ole, you're safe. Thank God those heathens didn't eat you. You look so thin; what did they do to you?"

"Don't worry, Auntie," Ole laughed. "Those people aren't heathens, they're mainly Catholics, and they don't eat people. They only shoot each other."

"You look so sick. Did they try to shoot you too?"

"I'm perfectly healthy . . . except that I stubbed my big toe one night," and he chortled.

"You should always wear shoes when you go overseas; I told you so, Ole. What's the matter? Why are you giggling?"

"The house looks so neat," Ole deftly changed the subject. "Thank you for looking after it; I know that I can always depend on you."

"Oh, Ole, I cleared and scrubbed the whole place from top to bottom; it was in such a mess. You need a wife to clean up after you. Why don't you get married? Yes, Ole, you were always messy, leaving things all over the place. You haven't changed, really you haven't." She paused to dry her face. "I threw out so much rubbish," she said in a tone that alarmed Ole.

"You did, did you? And what did you do with my books?"

"Books? What books?"

"Those exercise books I stacked in the corner back there."

"You mean those used-up filthy things? Oh, Ole, you shouldn't have kept your old schoolbooks. They collected so much dust and so many cockroaches."

"They're the most important things in my life. I cannot live without them," he declared and went looking for his books.

"They aren't here. What have you done with them?" he demanded rather crossly.

"Sit down, Ole, and let's talk like good Christians."

"No! Where are they?"

"Ole, you've always been a good boy. Sit down and have something to eat. You must be starving. What have they done to you?"

"Never mind that, I want my books!"

"Sit down and don't scream at me. That's a good boy. We're poor, you, me, the neighbours. And food is so expensive."

"Where are my books?"

"Toilet paper is beyond our reach. It used to be ten cents a roll."

"Yes, but what has that got to do with my books?"

"You didn't leave me any money when you went away, Ole. I had to eat and keep clean, and things are so expensive."

"I'm sorry, but where are my books?"

"Don't keep asking me that question, Ole, I'm trying to explain. I'm your only living aunt. And I'm very old and ready to go to Heaven. Don't hasten me along, please. Don't you think that I'm more important than any old book?"

"What did you do with them? Where are they?"

"Ole, I had no money for food; I had no money for toilet paper. I had to eat and keep clean. Stop looking at me like that. You frighten me so." She sniffed, blew her nose, then continued in a subdued tone. "I used some and sold the rest cheaply to the neighbours. They're poor, Ole, but they also have to be hygienic."

Ole stared at his aunt in disbelief. "No, no. You're pulling my leg: you didn't really sell my books for toilet paper. . . ."

"I did. Yes, yes, I did. I'm sorry but how could I have known they were so important?"

"Oh, my God!" Ole choked in anguish. He sat very still, breathing deeply, trying desperately to stop his arms from lashing out. Then slowly, very slowly, he mumbled, "Seven years' hard work down the bloody drain; shit!" Almost immediately the import of what he had uttered sank in and he burst into hysterical laughter, tears streaming down his cheeks. It was also then that the brilliant idea occurred to him. He reached out and embraced his aunt, apologising for his rudeness, promising never to do it again, and the old lady was so surprised at the transformation that she sobbed with tears of joy.

He recalled that he had Mr. Minte's government committed to $10,000 over five years. That was to be the start; he, Ole Pasifikiwei, whose books had gone down the drain, would henceforth go after the whales of the ocean. If he were to beg, he informed himself, he might as well do it on the grand scale. He therefore sent Mr. Minte an urgent letter and was soon rewarded with the arrival of Dr. Andrew Wheeler, a razor-sharp expert upon whose advice Ole instituted the National Council for Social, Economic, and Cultural Research, bagging chiefs, ministers of state, top-flight clergymen, wives of VIPs, and his old friend, Emi Bagarap, into honorary officeholding positions, with himself as full-time secretary. Then Dr. Wheeler devised a comprehensive four-year research programme and despatched professionally worded letters to INESCA, the Forge Foundation, the Friends of South Sea Natives, the Third World Conservation Commission, and the Konshu Fish and Forestry Institute for $400,000 funding.

A little later, and again with the skilled connivance of his indispensable Dr. Wheeler, Ole expanded by creating eighteen other national committees and councils with specific, aid-worthy objectives, and designed irresistibly attractive projects and schemes to be funded from international sources. And he capped it all by succeeding in getting his groups placed by the Great International Organisation on the list of the Two Hundred Least Developed Committees—those in need of urgent, generous aid.

After six years Ole had applied for a total of $14 million for his organisations, and his name had become well known in certain influential circles in Brussels, The Hague, Bonn, Geneva, Paris, London, New York, Washington, Wellington, Canberra, Tokyo, Peking, and Moscow, as well as in such regional laundry centres as Bangkok, Kuala Lumpur, Manila, Suva, and Noumea.

And the University of the Southern Paradise, whose wise, wily leaders saw in the man a great kindred talent that matched their own, bestowed upon him honorary doctoral degrees in Economics, Divinity, and Philosophy, although that learned institution had no philosophy of any kind, colour, or creed.

With fame and honour to his name, Ole Pasifikiwei immersed himself totally in the supreme task of development through foreign aid, relishing the twists and turns of international funding games. He has since shelved his original sense of self-respect and has assumed another, more attuned to his new, permanent role as a first-rate, expert beggar.

Note

This story appeared first as the final piece in the collection *Tales of the Tikongs* (Auckland: Longman Paul, 1983). Later the book was published by Penguin (1988); Beake House (Suva, 1993); and University of Hawai'i Press (Honolulu, 1994).

The Tuktuks

(EXCERPT FROM *Kisses in the Nederends*)

IN HIS VISION Seru saw the human body as a world in itself, a world inhabited by human-like creatures, the tuktuks, who organised themselves into tribes occupying territories located only in those parts of the body that contained organs and members, the most populous being lands in the lower erogenous regions. The arms and the legs were completely uninhabited and were visited only occasionally by a few intrepid hunters.

Tuktuk territories were grouped into upper and lower zones. Uppertuk tribes were those that occupied territories above the solar plexus, the Lowertuk tribes being those that lived from the abdomen down. Within each zone tribes were ranked according to their relative locations, above or below each other, the highest being those in the brain territories, the lowest those tuktuks who lived in the arse and the genitals.

It was the brain tribes who invented the ranking system, claiming that since they were the only ones who could see, hear, and smell things outside their body-world because of their commanding proximity to its major apertures, and that since they lived in the loftiest territories, far above the muck in the abdomen and the filth in the anal region, they were the best and cleanest tuktuks of all. They also believed that they were the cleverest since they had the good sense to live in the best part of the body-world. Uppertuks said that the worst, nastiest, dirtiest, smelliest, vilest, and generally the most beastly tuktuks were those who occupied the largely swampy territories of the arse. The most degenerate, horny, porno-brained, disgustingly obscene, perverted, and generally the most licentiously abandoned and loathsome were tuktuks who lived in the genital region.

Tuktuks subsisted on hunting ninongs, moose-like creatures that fed upon germs. They hunted with bows and arrows, spears, and boomerangs. Because ninongs lived in different environments and fed upon different types of germs, they varied greatly in kind, size, taste, and nutritional composition. The largest, tastiest, most nutritious, and therefore the most desired and prized were called nambawan ninongs, found only in the genital and anal territories. These heavenly creatures fed upon a special type of germ carried around by crab lice that inhabited the nethermost regions and nowhere else. It was natural therefore that anal and genital tuktuks called their parts of the body-world the Happy Hunting Grounds.

From the milk of the nambawan ninong was made a unique kind of cheese known as liebfraufromage, which had the aroma of the Red Rose of Sodom and the combined taste of twenty species of the Forbidden Fruit. Since this cheese was matured only by being buried for ten years in anal swamps, it was the exclusive product of the arse dwellers. Tuktuks were known to have sold their entire families down the drain for a single bite of the liebfraufromage.

Since tuktuks lived entirely on ninongs and ninong dairy products, it was absolutely necessary that they trade with each other in order to vary their diet and broaden their nutritional bases. The ninong trade was conducted and controlled by tribes in the brain region who had convinced all others of their superior organisational ability and business honesty. The main trade route to and from the brain region was the spinal cord, while the nerves served as roads that branched out to the rest of the body-world. Groups of ninong traders and their long lines of carriers were always trekking from one territory to another, buying and selling. There was fierce competition among these traders for the body-world distribution of liebfraufromage and nambawan ninongs.

Between the Uppertuks of the brain region and the Lowertuks of the anal and genital territories, there was little love lost. Much of their mutual animosity arose from the Uppertuk resentment of the fact that the things they wanted most were available only in the lowest regions. To obtain these products they had to go to those areas that to them were extremely unhealthy, filthy, and disgusting, and deal with tribes they considered far beneath them in intelligence and in physical and moral cleanliness. Through their familiarity with these lowest regions the brain Uppertuks had amassed a corpus of epithets that they freely hurled at Lowertuks, words directly related to the perceived characteristics of their environments. Uppertuks called Lowertuks arseholes, arselickers, buggers, bums, bullshitters, cocksuckers, cunts, fart faces, fuckwits, fucking this, fucking that, greedy guts, shitheads, turds, wankers, and other luridly offensive expressions. They characterised the mental and moral capacities of Lowertuks as piss weak and shit awful and their achievements as cockups. Lowertuk tattooists, cave painters, bone carvers, nose-flute players, chanters, and rain dancers were referred to as arty farty bullshit artists and poofters. In the department of invective, Lowertuks were at a distinct disadvantage. They could not use the words Uppertuks had invented for them because that would only demean their surroundings, of which they were extremely fond and proud. And since not one of them had ever been to the brain lands they knew next to nothing about life in the lofty region. All they could say of the Uppertuks was that they were dunderheads, thickheads, dummkopf, dumdum, bird-brained, nitwit, numbskull, scatter-brained, stupid, boofy, gormless, and other similarly inoffensive expressions.

Peace, stability, and prosperity prevailed in the body-world as long as ninongs abounded in every territory, each tribe limited its hunting to its own domain, no one tried to monopolise or in any way interfere with the ninong trade, and tuktuks confined their conflicts to exchanges of invective.

"Human beings are healthy only as long as the tuktuks inside them live in relative peace," Seru said. "But since there is no such thing as a perfect body-world, tuktuks are always in strife. Sometimes they confine their conflicts within a single territory, at times two or more regions are involved, and every now and then the whole body-world is at war. All diseases and illnesses in the human body and mind are caused by the messy tribal and intertribal relationships among the tuktuks.

"Oilei, your bottom's in a mess and your head's in turmoil because of long-drawn-out struggles between the arse and the brain tuktuks and among the brain dwellers themselves."

Many years before Oilei was stricken, Seru said, a ninong trading expedition headed by Bongotuk, chieftain of the smallest brain tribe, went to the anal region to get as many of the nambawan ninongs and as much liebfraufromage as he could for the initiation feast of his eldest daughter. While en route Bongotuk left the track on the only hill inside the region to attend to a call of nature. As he stepped a little distance into the bush he found a cave, the small mouth of which hid a huge natural chamber in which were stacked mounds of tuktuk skeletons. Bongotuk knew instantly that he had stumbled into the secret burial place of the anal tuktuks, the most sacred of their sacred grounds, which, until then, no outside tuktuk had ever seen. Being an Uppertuk who held the utmost contempt for Lowertuks, Bongotuk defecated in the cave without qualm. While squatting he picked up a shining round object and started bouncing it. He noticed that the cave was piled high with similar objects and said to himself, "I must take some for my little children." He stuffed many balls into his shoulder bag and left.

When the expedition returned home, Bongotuk bounced one ball in front of his children. As it bounced around it fell into the fireplace and exploded loudly, shattering a potful of ninongs. Bongotuk was amazed. He threw in another ball, which exploded with a terrific bang. Then he placed a trussed-up ninong near the fire and banged another ball, which killed the creature instantly. He thought for a while and, being a brainy tuktuk, searched for a strip of highly inflammable material, which he attached to another ball, lit it, and tossed the lot into the air. It went off and blew to pieces a large germ flying by.

Being a cruel and unscrupulous leader, Bongotuk saw in the balls the means to attain his long-held ambition to become the paramount chief of all the brain tribes and therefore control the entire ninong and liebfraufromage trade. Accordingly he sent his three sons and trusted minions secretly to the cave to fetch a large supply of balls, which he used to impose his dominance over all the hitherto-independent brain tribes and united them under a single rule for the first time ever. He had also despatched a strong force of warriors to take possession of the cave and prevent anyone else from gaining access.

The anal tuktuks protested vehemently against the desecration of their sacred ground. When these protests fell on deaf ears they mounted a series of attacks on the intruders, who easily repelled them with their explosives, killing a great number. Those who survived were hounded and slaughtered mercilessly, and their families massacred. In time Bongotuk subjugated the anal and genital tuktuks, forced them into breeding nambawan ninongs and manufacturing more liebfraufromage, levying a seventy percent tax in kind on all that they produced. Bongotuk also subjugated all the other tribes of the Lowertuk territories and was set on conquering the rest of the body-world. At the home front, Bongotuk's tribe had formed the ruling class of the new paramountcy and had reduced all the other tribes to the rank of carriers in the ninong trade. Bongotuk was hated both at home and abroad.

"Almost a year ago, just before you started feeling the pain in your arse," Seru addressed Oilei, "the anal tuktuks, instigated by their intolerable oppression and the continued desecration of their most sacred ground, rose in an open rebellion against their oppressors. From the beginning they have used guerrilla tactics because their weapons cannot match those of

Bongotuk's forces. They normally ambush Bongotuk's troops and retreat quickly into the deepest and densest swamps, where enemy warriors would not go on account of the filth and the stench. Using bows to fire explosive missiles, Uppertuks are bombarding these swamps, thus giving you the nasty pain in the arse.

"Even more recently the brain tuktuks from the oppressed tribes have taken advantage of the diversion caused by the Lowertuk rebellion to rise up and fight for their own liberation. They are set on overthrowing the ruling class. Bongotuk's warriors are bombarding the rebels, causing the nasty migraine that has doubled your suffering.

"The point is that there are two full-scale rebellions in your body-world. There's civil war in your brain and a Lowertuk guerrilla campaign against foreign domination. Your pains will persist as long as these conflicts remain unresolved. You will have even more pain if the other Lowertuk tribal territories rise against Bongotuk."

"That's the most fantastic thing I've ever heard, Seru," Oilei marvelled. "The rebellions sound exactly like what you hear from the BBC news service every day."

Note

This excerpt is from chapter 6 of the novel *Kisses in the Nederends,* published by Penguin (NZ), Auckland, 1987. Reprinted by University of Hawai'i Press, Honolulu, 1995.

Oilei and Babu

(EXCERPT FROM *Kisses in the Nederends*)

IT WAS LATE in the afternoon when Bulbul arrived. He emerged from the driver's seat, walked to the other side, and opened the passenger door. A tall, elderly, lean, white-haired and white-bearded man wearing a dhoti and carrying a battered briefcase stepped out, took a deep breath, and, escorted by Bulbul, walked lightly up the path towards the house.

Oilei watched all this from the open doorway, surprised at seeing his friend acting the chauffeur. But Bulbul, never known to kowtow to the wealthy and the powerful, always deferred reverentially towards holy men of all religions.

"I have brought the great yogi and sage, Babu Vivekenand, who most generously and graciously offers you his services. Babu, this is my best friend, Oilei Bomboki, of whom I have already told you," Bulbul introduced them stiffly.

"The Creator of all things showers his blessings upon you," Babu said. "I have heard much about you and must say that I have been very impressed. I and my organisation owe you a great deal. Without knowing it, you have rendered us a great service. No. Do not ask questions; things will be revealed in due course. It is an immense pleasure for me to have this opportunity to be of some use to you. Shall we go inside? Thank you.

"A good house you have here," Babu complimented as he walked in. "Very well ventilated. Ventilation is a necessary feature of any house. There should always be plenty of moving air in confined spaces. Aaah, chairs. . . . No thank you, I prefer the floor. The surfaces on which one stands, sits, or lies must always be firm and solid. Helps to keep the spine straight, thus encouraging good breathing and circulation."

Babu lowered himself on the floor and effortlessly assumed a lotus sitting posture. Oilei and Bulbul followed suit but sat cross-legged facing him. The sage kept his counsel for a while before he began with the authority of a physician in his surgery.

"Please remove the handkerchief from your face. Thank you. I can see what our friend meant when he gave an account of your problem. All problems in the world are connected, however disparate they may appear on the surface. There are no unrelated or unique problems. We isolate them from each other only because it is easier to deal with them separately. Therein lies an even bigger connected problem. Inasmuch as we deal with reality in piecemeal ways, in the long run we never find lasting solutions. What we always produce are short-term solutions that generate even bigger and more intractable problems.

"Take your illness, for example. Because you thought that only your anus was in trouble, you tried to find a cure for it. Yesterday, as our friend here informed me, you discovered that it was connected with problems elsewhere in the body, although the Rovoni expert misunderstood the real nature of the causes. There are no tuktuks. But your limited and distorted understanding of the larger ramifications of your anal problem is nevertheless evidence of the relatedness of things. We talk of things as if they were separate and unique. There is only a single reality, of which we and everything else are manifestations. We are united in the One Infinite, the Absolute Ground of Being. There are no separate existences. Keep this in mind while we deal with your particular case.

"The problem with your anus is rooted in the inherent human tendency to isolate and then divide manifestations of the One Infinite, in this instance, the human body, into different parts and assign to each of them different values. You and most of the rest of humanity look at parts of the body and say that some are good and beautiful and others bad and repulsive. You're proud of some and ashamed of others. You would not, for example, discuss the anus on the same level as the eyes. The body itself is a unity and together with the mind and the soul forms a larger unity of the being. You can go on from there indefinitely. The whole phenomenon is very complex and requires a great deal of intellectual effort to fully comprehend. We shall not go into it here, for most of it cannot be articulated through words. You will realise it more and more as you progress with yoga.

"All parts of the human body are of equal value. But you have, in your limited perception of reality, viewed them very differently. People have composed countless songs about the beauty of the eyes, the lips, the hands, and the breast. But there is no music, no poetry, that extols the merits of the anus. You can flaunt your face and other parts of your body, but if you dare bare your anus in public you will be apprehended for obscenity.

"You should already have noticed that I use the word 'anus' and not 'arse,' which is loaded with the most repulsive connotations associated with a part of the body that is as good, as beautiful, as worthy of lyrical poetry as any. The anus is the most maligned, most unjustly loathed and abused part of the body. When people behave atrociously they are called arseholes. It is extremely reprehensible to compare the innocent anus with the dregs of society. Thoroughly obnoxious people are often called stinking arseholes. Yet they could easily be called stinking armpits or smelly mouths. These parts of the body surely discharge odours as pungent as those that come from any other parts. Also, filthy people are called dirty arseholes. The anus is as clean as any part of the body. And if you think objectively, you will see that the anus is always washed more thoroughly than any part of the body. Most people wash it too vigorously when showering, as if they were punishing it for being there, or trying to rub it off. But the anus has the right to be where it is, and to be treated with respect and love. We treat our heads with respect and call our leaders heads. We could, with equal felicity, call them anuses.

"The anus is like the lower orders of society. It does the most unpleasant jobs and no one would like their daughters to marry garbage collectors. It is class prejudice of the worst order. The great teacher, Jesus of Nazareth, once told his disciples to behave towards the least members of society as they behaved towards him. We must behave likewise towards our anuses. It is therefore necessary to review your whole attitude towards the anus. You must change and be convinced in your being that the anus is good, beautiful, lovable, and respectable.

"You may recall that not many years ago Prime Minister Morarji Desai admitted to drinking his own piddle. Half the world was horrified and repulsed; the other half laughed. Almost everyone missed the great symbolic significance of the Prime Minister's behaviour; and that is, no part or product of the human being and therefore no human being is inherently repulsive and detestable. We must therefore bestow on the anus the dignity it has long been denied and restore it to its rightful and equal place among the honoured parts of our bodies. Only when you love and respect the rights of the lowliest member of your own body can you really love and respect the rights of the least members of your society. Mahatma Gandhi launched India on a new road by calling the untouchables 'children of God' and giving them equal rights. We must do more by adding to the revered triumvirate of the body, mind, and soul, the hitherto lowly anus.

"It is only when you are able to lovingly and respectfully kiss your own anus, and those of your fellow human beings, that you will know you have purified yourself of all obscenities and prejudices, and have overcome your worst fears and phobias. You will then be able to see with utmost clarity the true nature of beauty, which is the essence of the unity and equality of all things. For while you assign different values to different parts of your body and consider some of them dirty, disgusting, and shameful, you will continue to assign the same values but with even greater intensity to similar parts of other people's bodies. That is, of course, a short route to hating and loathing them. Only when you treat every part of your body equally can you begin your journey towards true love. And once there, your life will harmonise with the One Infinite, and all your pains and agues will disappear. Sickness, disease, and death strike us because of disharmonies in our existence. But when we synchronise our lives with the Eternal Programme of the Universe, we will live forever.

"You can see now what I mean by the interconnectedness of all life and what happens when these connections are weakened or broken. I could continue along this line but it suffices for the moment that you have seen the broader context of your problem. There are practical steps you must take to reconcile your anus with the rest of your being and with the One Infinite so that you may be cured of your illness. These steps consist of two sets of yoga exercises.

"The first is relatively easy to master. The object is to enable you to see your anus closely for so often and for such prolonged periods that it is not strange and disgusting any more. It will be as normal and familiar to you as are the palms of your hands; and to your nose, it will be as the fresh bud of spring. You will also marvel at the beauty of its structure and formation and at the rhythm of its movements. At the end of all this, you will have written a poem, 'Ode to My Lovely Anus,' which you may put to music and perform to rapturous audiences."

Babu then paused and rose to demonstrate what he wanted Oilei to achieve at the end of the first series of yoga exercises. He took off his dhoti, folded it neatly and placed it aside, bent down very easily from the waist, hands behind him, placed his head between the unbent knees, parted his buttocks, and looked up at his anus. Oilei was enraptured by the old man's suppleness.

The yogi returned to his sitting position after he had put on his clothes.

"The second series of exercises will enable you to reach your anus," he said as he stretched on his back and raised his legs and waist so that they were perpendicular to the rest of his body. Then he lifted his torso so that only the base of his spine remained on the floor. Following this, he spread his legs wide apart and bent his head until his nose touched his buttocks. Then slowly and gracefully he disengaged his head, lowered his body, and returned to the sitting position.

"This second series of exercises will enable you to do what I have just done. They are not easy but if you do them conscientiously and properly you should be able to reach your goal in six to twelve months. You must remember that at your age your bones and muscles are stiff. But everything is possible given concentration and the will to succeed. You obviously had these qualities in your younger days; let us hope for the sake of your anus that you still have them today.

"When you get to the stage of being able to reach your anus with your nose, you will kiss it several times and, maintaining that position, meditate on it. You will then easily dispose of your revulsion and free yourself from the attitudes that inhibit your perception of the love that dwells in the unity of all things, and you will attain the state of harmony that will, by its very existence, cure you of all maladies. From that point on you will progress to higher things such as kissing other people's anuses. But you must obtain their consent first, and do it in complete privacy or you will be in trouble with the law. When this practice becomes widespread we will be in a position to press for law reform; and we will get reform just as other previously abhorrent practices have been legalised."

Oilei could not understand all this; the very idea of bussing his own and other people's arseholes was most absurd and disgusting.

"Babu," he said hesitantly, "you said what you have said, but will you really act on it, like kissing your own arse, er, anus?"

"Of course. I've done it many times. Watch me carefully."

And the great sage disrobed, stretched out on his back, raised the lower and upper parts of his body as before, spread his legs wide apart, used both hands to spread his buttocks, and buried his nose in it. He repeated the action several times in the most dignified and graceful manner before he put his dhoti back on and resumed his lotus position.

Utterly fascinated by the performance, Oilei said in all sincerity, "Babu, will you kiss my anus?"

"Certainly, and most willingly. I had expected that request, as a matter of fact."

Oilei disrobed and bared his bottom at the holy man, not quite certain that he would do it. But Babu rose into a kneeling position, parted Oilei's buttocks delicately, and in a reverential and sacramental manner, placed his nose inside. He drew back and repeated the action three more times before he resumed his lotus posture, saying, "I have kissed your blessed anus with love and respect. If the presidents of the United States and the Soviet Union do likewise at their next summit meeting, there will be no more threat of nuclear annihilation and there will be set an example for all the leaders of the world to emulate. As in most things we must begin from the top down. When the top meets the bottom, there will be eternal peace."

Oilei noticed a change in the old man's demeanour as Babu paused before launching himself into something that seemed to have troubled him profoundly.

"The anus, as you have now seen, is neither revolting nor obscene. The most revolting and obscene thing we live with today is the threat of nuclear annihilation. It is obscene because of the spectre of destruction that it presents to all of us, but more so because it perpetuates, for as long as nuclear weapons exist, the fears, suspicions, and hatreds that blind us to the beauty of creation; that is, the love, trust, and respect that we can have for one another.

"Those who possess and control the most dangerous means of destruction have condemned themselves to live with increasing paranoia that breeds psychopathic behaviour; this may very well lead to their own undoing and the undoing of us all. They have spread that paranoia to their neighbours, satellites, and client states. Every country that deals intimately with them has caught their incurable disease. The balance of terror they hold out to be the mainstay of peace means increasingly terrified populations, which know peace only as a precarious state of no war. Balance of terror is the most obscene invention of the human mind. Those who live in it live in terror disguised as vigilance and will never find serenity of mind and the true love of all life that are preconditional for lasting peace. Those who control the most destructive weapons, those who allow their territory to harbour such weapons, and those who are directly and intensively influenced by them, are progressively psychopathically violent in every sense of the word. More and more they admire and worship violence and vengeful Ramboism.

"You are slightly fortunate in the South Pacific in that your relationships with them are not yet quite as intimate as others'. You must therefore keep them at arm's length so that you at least may maintain a semblance of civility and humanity that will make your conditions bearable. The purveyors of the balance of terror are sending their emissaries, their nuclear ships and submarines to your shores to draw you into the vortex of their paranoia, for they can neither conceive of nor tolerate the idea that there are human beings who are genuinely free and wish to remain free of the self-inflicted fears that are undermining the foundations of their societies. You must remember that the dinosaurs did not kill each other off; each was its own murderer.

"Only one country in your region has been sane and courageous enough to tell the purveyors of terror to keep their madness to themselves. You must join this country and try to join with men and women in the fear-racked, violent societies who are struggling to bring back some measure of sanity to our collective existence.

"One way of contributing to world peace, and this is where your seemingly unrelated and unique personal problem is in fact connected to global issues of great moment, is to spread the gospel that every part of the human body is beautiful and sacred in the eyes of the gods. We must begin from ourselves, from the lowest organs of our bodies, before we expand elsewhere. We must be able to celebrate the anus as we celebrate the mind and the heart, and from there to proclaim that in the realm of the One Infinite we do not call people arseholes, buggers, cunts, dildos, fuckwits, poofters, shits, turds, or wankers. We must greet, love, and dance with each other in the middle of our zones of taboo, for we have not created any real taboos, only the fears and phobias that we, in our limitless capacity for self-delusion, have swept to the boundaries of our cherished conventions, where they remain to haunt us into insanity and violence.

"For you, Oilei, learn to love your anus and those of your neighbours and never again call them arseholes. Kiss your anus and theirs, and you are on the road towards contributing to the healing of our collective self."

The great sage paused and extracted a manila folder from his briefcase and handed it to Oilei.

"In that are copies of the exercises that you will do every morning. It will be months before you reach your goal, but always keep in mind that long-term solutions are the best.

"Finally, you will from now on stop swearing and blaspheming. That will help to clear the fog in your mind and the stains on your soul. Some time after I leave, you will see a miracle."

That evening Oilei was in bed, lost in his recollection of all that Babu had said and done, when Makarita tiptoed in, touched his groin, and whispered loudly, "Hey champ, let's do it. . . . Shhh, cocky, did you hear me?" and tugged at the jackhammer.

"What?"

"I said let's fuck."

"My dear Rita," Oilei spoke from a great distance, "we no longer use that word. It fogs the mind and stains the soul. You should have said, 'Let us persuade our respective members to engage in a sacrament of love.' That's the cleanest way of putting it."

"Engage . . . our members . . . in a sacra . . . oh shit! That's a load of crap!"

"We do not use those words either. Faeces are good, wholesome by-products that are essential to agriculture."

"Agriculture? What's that got to do with turd?"

"Rita my darling . . ."

"Don't my-darling me, you crazy arsehole!"

"Those aren't terms of endearment . . ."

"Endearment! What's wrong with you? Have you lost your fucking balls?"

"My sweet spouse . . ."

"Sweet spouse, for Chrissake! Talk sense! Do you or don't you want a screw?"

"Rita, Rita my beloved. Your name rings of the sounds of Eden. By all means flap your wings, spread your limbs and shortly we shall be in Paradise engaging our respective members . . ."

"O Lord. You've really gone cuckoo this time. Forget that I asked you. Forget it! You're so romantic! I'm off sex for good! Do you hear me? I may as well join a convent!" Rita rushed out weeping with frustration.

Oilei remained still, contemplating the ceiling. He had been a changed man since Babu the yogi anointed his anus. He lowered his eyes slowly and saw his reflection in the mirror. To his great delight his nose was no longer pink. He checked his bottom; it too had changed colour back to normal. It must have been a result of that kiss of love and respect, he told himself as he drifted off to sleep.

In the early hours of the morning, Makarita woke up to answer a call of nature. She entered the bedroom because she was surprised that the light was still on so late; Oilei was never a night owl. What she saw then convinced her that her husband had really gone around the bend. He was lying there fast asleep while his mouth was frozen in an act of kissing something. Most probably something disgusting, Makarita told herself.

A few hours later she stepped into the lounge to observe Oilei doing some strange exercises she had never seen before. In fact, since she had known him she had not seen him doing any physical exercises. Perhaps he did not need to, because hard work on the farm had kept him superbly trim. She guessed that he was exercising because of the long period of inactivity since his illness began.

"What're you on to now?" she asked.

"I'm doing yoga, my love."

"Yoga?" Makarita had never heard that word before. Neither had Oilei until he met Babu.

"It's a special kind of exercise that enables people to do great things."

"You're not taking up boxing again, are you?"

"Goodness gracious me, no, my beloved. It's something far more significant. Boxing is nothing by comparison. It's something that will contribute tremendously to peaceful intercourse . . ."

"You wouldn't have one with me last night . . ."

"I tried to approach it cleanly but you wouldn't listen. Anyway, what I mean is that what I'm doing will lead to something that will promote the advancement of peace in the world."

"I don't understand."

"The first series of yoga exercises will enable me to look at my anus."

"Your what?" Makarita couldn't believe what she was hearing, especially her husband's avoidance of crude words.

"My anus, you know. It's a clean word that . . ."

"I prefer arse. But why would anyone want to look up his arsehole?"

"So that I may love and respect it."

"Love and respect your own . . . no. You're pulling my leg."

"Far from it, my sweet spouse, I . . ."

"Don't call me that again, you idiot. Makes me feel like I'm some spilled lemonade. Yuk!"

"Far from it, my dear. You see, when I love and respect my anus, I will kiss it."

"Kiss your own arse? Sweet Mother of God!!"

"Most certainly yes," Oilei asserted with the conviction of the born-again street corner preacher. "And afterwards, I will love and respect your anus and kiss it too."

"Kiss my arse you will, will you? Never!!"

"But that's not the end of the matter, you see. The time will come when you will love and respect my anus and kiss it too, because . . ."

"Me kissing your bleeding arsehole? I will do no such disgusting thing!! Never!! Urrgh. You make me sick!!"

"Oh, you will, my beloved, when you see the beauty of . . ."

"Your filthy thing down there beautiful? You're out of your fucking nut!!"

Makarita shrieked with laughter of the kind that comes only from those on the verge of a nervous breakdown. Realising what was happening, she checked herself. She must keep her sanity. Oilei was already over the edge.

"You kiss mine, I kiss yours. That's what you're aiming for, aren't you? What will the neighbours think?"

"Never mind the neighbours, my beloved. I will kiss their anuses too, and they will kiss mine . . ."

"And mine into the bargain, I suppose. So we're going to have a mass orgy, are we?"

"It will not be an orgy. It'll be the new eucharist. And if the presidents of the United States and the Soviet Union . . ."

Oilei stopped abruptly when Makarita, for no conceivable reason, began to shriek again and then crashed on the floor and lay still. He lifted her onto the divan, tucked a cushion under her head, checked her breathing, pulse, and eyes, and slapped her lightly on the face several times. She opened her eyes, registered what she saw, and passed out a second time. Oilei slapped her some more until she came to. This time utter horror and disgust stared into his face. She instinctively tightened her legs together, tucked one hand under her bottom, and pushed Oilei away with the other.

"Go away. Don't touch me. Don't come near me." She rose and edged away from him, still protecting her behind. She opened the front door and disappeared.

Oilei shrugged his shoulders and resumed his exercise.

Note

This excerpt is chapter 7 of the novel *Kisses in the Nederends,* published by Penguin (NZ), Auckland, 1987. Reprinted by University of Hawai'i Press, Honolulu, 1995.

Epeli Hau'ofa Interviewed by Subramani

THIS INTERVIEW took place in Suva in September 1988 at the University of the South Pacific where both were teaching, Epeli Hau'ofa in the Department of Sociology and Subramani in the Department of Literature and Language. Subramani provided a set of thought-provoking written questions; Hau'ofa then produced written answers. Initially the interview appeared in the New Zealand literary journal *Landfall 169* (vol. 43, no. 1, 1989, 35–51). The novel *Kisses in the Nederends* had first been published by Penguin (NZ) in 1987. The University of Hawai'i Press edition (1995) includes the *Landfall* interview.

SUBRAMANI: *I have no difficulty reading* Kisses in the Nederends *independently of biography—fiction should speak for itself—though, of course, for our purpose biography should be interesting. I'm reminded of Sainte-Beuve's often quoted comment: "Literature, literary creation, is not distinct or separable, for me, from the rest of the man. . . . I may taste a work, but it is difficult for me to judge it independently of my knowledge of the man himself." Perhaps because I was aware of the personal distress well before the novel came into being, I can see how that experience has provided the substance and structure for the novel. The question I want to ask is how free do you feel to divulge information about the particular experience that inspired the creation of this novel?*

HAU'OFA: I have no problem with the question. As in all things Pacific, information and misinformation about my little malady are already public, so it's no use being demure. One must set the record straight. I'll give the official version anyway. Straight from the horse's arse, as they say in polite circles.

There is no doubt in my mind about the fact that the inspiration for the work, its "substance and structure" as you put it, came from a very painful personal experience. I'll give a fairly detailed account, for the substance, structure, and some of the chronology of events closely reflect my own experience. Of course, taking full advantage of literary licence I distorted and exaggerated things out of all reasonable proportions for the sake of a good story and dramatisation of certain ideas about behaviour and society in general.

I first experienced the pain in Tonga in 1981. My doctor opened its source and drained it. About a year later the pain, an excruciating one, recurred and the same doctor performed the same operation. Unfortunately he did not tell me anything more about it so I assumed that it was a simple boil in the bum, and boils are very common in the tropics. I had dozens of them before I turned twenty. I must also admit that in 1982 I had no knowledge whatsoever about fistulae that grow as a result of anal infection. I did not know that this was a major cause of what is popularly known as "pain in the arse." Tongans have a word for it, *kahi,* but I thought that it referred only to piles and I had never had piles before. Anyway I dismissed it as a common or garden variety tropical boil, except that I had never had it right up there where it could do a lot of damage. But there was something very peculiar about my "boil." After the second operation the wound refused to heal as normal boil openings do. It remained where it was as a living sore, and every now and then I had attacks of pain, which remained for a while before it subsided.

One day I told my neighbour about it. He listened and left, only to return shortly with an old man whom he introduced as a specialist in curing anything that goes wrong in people's bottoms. The old man went straight to business. He asked me where the pain was. I told him it was in the left buttock. He looked straight into my eyes as he massaged my left knee for about five seconds. "That's all for now," he said. "At eight tomorrow morning sit in the lounge, bare your left knee, and we'll continue with our treatment. Do it at the same time every morning for one week." He left without saying anything else.

On the following morning I sat in the lounge and waited for him. He did not turn up that day or the following days. A week later, he reappeared with my neighbour. He looked straight into my eyes and very politely accused me of not baring my left knee every morning as I was supposed to. (I had already complained to my neighbour some days earlier that the old man never returned for treatment.) I replied that I had been waiting every morning for him but he never turned up. The old man smiled faintly and said nothing. Then my neighbour explained that the instruction was for me to bare my knee at home at a certain time every day while the specialist did the healing massage long-distance, sitting in his own house. This was said in all seriousness, and in a similar vein I was instructed to do precisely as I was told, starting the following morning. I only just managed to keep a straight face. It was my first brush with hocus pocus bush medicine.

So I lived with my festering sore and pain, and in early 1983 I brought them over with my family to work at the campus in Suva. They got worse: the sore grew in size and the pain returned to haunt me more frequently than before. Eventually I went to the doctor, who explained what the problem was all about. He also told me that it needed a very careful and delicate operation but advised that it must be done either in New Zealand or Australia or America. Fiji lacked the expertise and facilities for it. He knew of one or two people who were operated on here with the result that they became permanently incontinent. "You don't want to carry a potty everywhere for the rest of your life, do you?" he asked unnecessarily.

I was most discouraged, especially since I had no money to travel to New Zealand, let alone pay for the operation and hospitalisation. I also dreaded taking drugs since I fell into a state of nearly fatal anaphylactic shock in 1982 and suspected that I was fatally allergic to some kinds of drugs. So I started looking for alternative medicine. And to my delight there was no lack of curers and healers—with herbs for taking orally, leaves for steaming and smoking the rump, massages, acupuncture needles for sticking into one's sensitivities, prayers and incantations, and whatnot. I must have gone through the skilled hands of dozens of practitioners of ancient medicine. I must have spent almost as much as I needed for treatment overseas.

But it was all to no avail. The pain intensified into an unbelievable agony. The sore discharged so continuously that I had to wear cotton pads, and when those did not suffice I graduated to Modess and suchlike. It was utterly ridiculous. I felt like a permanently menstruating female mandrill. I also took a thick cushion to work because it was well nigh impossible to sit on any chair. And when that failed me, a considerate friend recommended the inflated tube of a wheelbarrow tyre. It had its merits. It is the right size for normal human bottoms; it bounces; and it does not touch the sore, which remains suspended in the hollow. So I duly bought one and carried it in an oversized handbag wherever I went. Eventually it not only failed me, it nearly damned well killed me one day when it bounced a shot of searing pain straight up into my brain. I stopped using it. In April or May 1985 when I was more or less bedridden I seriously entertained the idea of getting a leg-traction machine to get my lower half suspended in the air. But that was impossible without going into hospital. It was then that I realised I must go overseas for treatment. Things happened fast after that belated decision. I easily obtained financial assistance from the university, flew to New Zealand, and had a successful operation done. Somewhere down below there is a most artistically carved scar that looks like a Polynesian face tattoo. Every time I thought of it I could see the fantastic doctor who created it. I made a reference to it on page 120 of the novel.

My summary account of what happened to me over a period of four years shows something about the structure and substance of the novel. But it does not bring out forcefully enough the reality of physical and mental agony that I experienced. Throughout the later part of the period I moaned and groaned and also laughed at the absurdity of my suffering. The best form of relief during that period came from earthy jokes and the ribbing I got from Fijian secretaries, typists, and cleaners at our school, all of them women. Laughing at problems, especially seemingly intractable ones, is a feature of many Pacific cultures. For me, this capacity for laughter, for grabbing moments of joy in the midst of suffering, is one of the most attractive things about our islands. We laugh and we cry and we often do them simultaneously.

I tried to reflect some of this in the novel. I also tried to give some indication of what it feels like when one suffers acute and sustained physical pain. And when such agony afflicts one for several years, it affects the whole of one's life. One becomes obsessed with it; one becomes testy and cranky and rude towards those one loves. My family went through a horrendous period but somehow survived. The flow of obscenities out of Oilei's mouth is partly an attempt by me to describe vividly the intensity of his agony, the psychological effect it has on him, and the social consequences that his erratic behaviour wreaks upon his family, friends, and everyone who comes into contact with him. Yet through it all Oilei's family and friends stay by him, as mine did by me. They suffer and laugh with him, as mine did with me. These were some of the things I wanted to bring out. There were others as well.

Finally, writing the novel turned out to be psychological therapy. My operation rid me of an intense physical pain, but it didn't do much else besides. I was still psychologically obsessed, and my temper, though improved, was still short. But most of this evaporated after I had written the novel. I'm more equable than I was between 1981 and 1985, and I use obscene language much less frequently than before I wrote the novel. Oilei does too.

SUBRAMANI: *I'm interested in your understanding of laughter—you have mentioned laughter a number of times. Is there such a thing as "Pacific laughter"?*

HAU'OFA: I really don't know. One has to do a lot of research to arrive at an informed answer. Like other aspects of human behaviour, what people laugh at or about is culturally conditioned. A group may laugh at or about things that another group may not. And it is common in the Pacific that a group may laugh at things about themselves but if an outsider laughs at the very same things, the group may not at all be amused. There are all kinds of in-jokes that are exclusive. Tongans have a fantastic sense of humour, very similar to Fijians and other groups in Melanesia that I know of. Now the sorts of things that I laugh at or about in *Tales* are the kinds of things that Tongans laugh about. They love playing with words. Yet many Tongans are not very enamoured of *Tales,* which is considered by many to be about Tonga. That is only a tiny part of the truth. Those of my compatriots who are indignant about my work feel that I have made what we laugh at about ourselves known to others. We know and admit our absurdity but we should not let others know. Outsiders don't understand us and they would think that we're a bunch of idiots. The feeling is not uncommon in the Pacific.

There are also groups in the Pacific whom other groups think to be uptight and quick to take offence. When you are with such groups you have to be careful; even though you may joke with them, you may easily offend them unintentionally. Tongans and Fijians may rib each other mercilessly and merrily, but would be on their guard when dealing with some others, those who seem to have a strong sense of propriety and are much more openly defensive about their honour, their personal and group dignity, especially in the company of outsiders. Although they may have a great sense of humour and joke readily with others, in general they are relatively easily pricked.

Having said that, the people that I know best, Tongans, Fijians, and coastal and small island Papua New Guineans, have an enormous propensity for laughter—they laugh at the drop of a hat. Someone told me a story of a Tongan family who took shelter in their small, low cookhouse after their dwelling was razed by a particularly vicious hurricane. Every member of the family hung onto the lower parts of the roof to prevent it from being blown away. They laughed and joked for hours about the situation they were in, while outside the hurricane was doing its best to destroy them. One of the things I dislike about going to serious movies in our islands is the damned audience. They always laugh uproariously at the wrong things and ruin the movie. It's like when I first went to Australia. Fresh out of the boondocks, I tended to laugh merrily at all sorts of things—and not infrequently someone would ask indignantly, "What are you laughing at?" I almost lost my sense of humour trying to be civilised; but fortunately I never got quite civilised.

SUBRAMANI: *Did the writing of this novel lead you to any profound observations on the relationship between personal suffering (sickness) and man's creative capacities, or on Freudian theories about the roots of art?*

HAU'OFA: I don't know. I have long been aware of the relationship between personal suffering and creativity. I would not have written *Kisses* without firsthand experience of the particular kind of physical agony that I have told you about. An interesting thing is that I did not think of writing anything about it while I went through the experience. It was after the cure that the idea occurred. In fact I got it almost as soon as I left the hospital. I remember having dinner soon after my release when I mentioned to my Auckland host and hostess that I might just write a book about "pain in the arse." We all laughed; it was a joke; but it stuck. At the time I was almost due for a long leave, which I had decided to spend on writing. I had a number of possibilities but I had not made any decision. Anyway, the freedom from pain was such a relief and a joy that I laughed at the idea of writing a book about the experience. I also realised at the time that as far as I knew, very little sustained writing had been devoted to that part of the body. I had not come across nor heard of anyone who had written an entire novel about the anus. This might well have been a consequence of my limited knowledge of literature. Of course, Freud had written about anal fixation, but his work was scientific and clinical.

This realisation, and it might well have been a false one, that I was contemplating writing something rare or new, that is, an entire novel about the workings of the most despised part of the human body, gave me a tremendous boost to wade into it, so to speak. Personal suffering provided the initial inspiration, the substance, and the structure; the excitement of venturing into relatively virgin territory was the motor that propelled me into it. Once I started thinking seriously about it and planning the approach, I realised that I was treading on an area of taboo, at least for our island societies. But I was already so committed that I pranced merrily ahead regardless of consequences.

I began discovering a world of wonderfully weird possibilities. One of these was that of writing something grotesque, obscene, disgusting, and utterly silly, but doing it in such a way that I could get away with it by having it brought out by a reputable publishing house. That was a challenge for one's ingenuity. (I had already been approached by a highly respected publisher who was interested in my work after he read *Tales.*) With the world, or at least the Pacific Ocean, as a playground, I wrote and wrote and sent an early draft to Penguin more than half-expecting it to be rejected out of hand. But to my joyous surprise the publisher urged me to go ahead, with extremely useful comments and suggestions. Thus encouraged I went into it with even more gusto than before, pushing my luck to the limits. I shall always be grateful to Geoff Walker, managing editor of Penguin (NZ), for his encouragement and his decision to publish my work. What I have been trying to say is that behind a person's creativity are many factors, not just one like personal suffering.

SUBRAMANI: *Recognising that your intention is one thing and what you in fact achieved is another, would you like to comment on how your primary intention changed at any stage and, if you have gone back to the published novel, do you find what you created is what you set out to accomplish? Is it more or less than what you intended? I suppose what I want to know is to what extent do you work instinctively? Are there things in the novel that you discover now that you thought weren't there?*

HAU'OFA: The short answer to these questions is that the book is to a large extent what I intended it to be. As I have already said, the structure, much of the substance, and some of the chronology reflect my actual experience. But there was, again, not just a single intention. Other intentions arose during the process of writing and rewriting. I believe they were all related one way or another.

I initially gave myself at least a year to write and polish the book.

My first one, *Tales of the Tikongs,* took about four years. I really worked on that one, polishing and refining the stories, and since it was my first attempt at prose fiction I tried consciously to develop a distinctive style and a voice of my own. With the novel, I finished it in six months. I was going to spend at least another six months to polish and refine it, but I decided against that because I would have eliminated most of the profanities and obscenities and so cleaned it up as to make it smell like a brand new hospital. The book would have come out as a work of "acceptable humour," as a nice English lady once told me about *Tales.* I intended *Kisses* to come out very differently; I wanted it raw, not cooked.

Now, the actual details and working out of events in the book were to a large degree things that emerged as I wrote. I would have near-total control had I written it as a realistic autobiographical novel. But since all the characters and events were imaginative, I had far less control over them as they tended to be elusive and follow their own logic. I created the characters and more or less set them on particular paths; but once they came alive they became fairly independent and I had to follow them and try to steer them, sometimes successfully and sometimes unsuccessfully. And sometimes I got lost myself. I found out during the writing that I was living in a different but somehow real world full of strange people, not unlike those with whom I lived as an anthropologist. I grew fond of them, and although they did outrageous things, I did not dislike any single person in that world. I remember writing to someone close to me after I had submitted the manuscript, saying that I had just returned from a long journey to another country; lived among a crazy and most lovable people; that I was the first stranger to go there; that I felt somewhat melancholic because I was just about to lead other strangers to it; and that that world would no longer be just mine and theirs. The experience, though real, was rather eerie because it was all in the mind; but perhaps it is not an uncommon experience among those who create worlds of imagination. Anyway, I had created what I now think to be a lovable lot of people, and that was not intended. They demanded to be treated as human and humane beings. I intentionally distorted and caricatured them and made them comical. But they refused to be made into anything less than human. This perhaps says something about the resilience of the human spirit. And it is something that I've only just found out.

What I have just said has led me to another discovery: one may intend to do certain things without conscious awareness of the intention. Before I wrote the book I was aware of the fact that the solutions to the major and long-term problems in the South Pacific must be global in nature. When I returned to the islands in 1975 I thought that most of the important national problems could be solved simply by national measures. Thus in Tonga I strongly advocated the idea of living within our means, of looking at our own cultural heritage for appropriate solutions, and so forth. My very small publication, *Our Crowded Islands,* is a product of this kind of thinking. No one wanted to know what I was saying. I soon found out the reason for it: our economy, society, culture, and indeed our very existence are not fenced in by our national boundaries. We are inextricably part of larger entities: the Pacific region and, more important, the world economy. The solutions to all the major problems in our islands lie in regional and ultimately in wider international cooperation (even if this means struggle) and not so much in our own small and narrow local efforts.

Conversely, our very existence as small and isolated groups of people occupying a vast surface of the earth, like human groups occupying the scattered oases of the Sahara, is our unbolted backdoor. The result is that our Pacific region is the favourite ground for weapons testing by all major powers of the world, toxic waste disposal, and rapacious ocean resources exploitation.

All this underlies my sentiments against the romantic neotraditionalism of elements of our societies, championed by those who are reaping the juiciest fruits that the world capitalist economy gives. These champions tend to wail by the banks of the River of Babylon and proclaim undying devotion to what they have abandoned. They are in the good company of Euro-American romanticists whom they forever denounce. At least Hollywood's makers of Pacific paradise movies were honest cynics who did what they did for money and nothing else.

These were thoughts that went through my mind in 1985 before and during the writing of the novel; and they still haunt me today. The solutions to our major problems must be international because these problems arise from global movements of money, men, and machinery. And it has only just occurred to me that Oilei's search for the ultimate solution to his problem reflects those thoughts quite closely. He tries local dottores, an acupuncturist, and medical officers to no avail. Then he goes regional (to a New Zealand hospital, that is) too late. But he is at last healed by the world Third Millenium Movement.

SUBRAMANI: *At what stage did you realise that the comic brutalities on Bomboki's anus could work as an extended metaphor? Is it a metaphor?*

HAU'OFA: Yes it is a metaphor for society and for everything else I could think of. I realised that it was a metaphor quite soon after I had started thinking about the outline of the book. So I placed it at the centre of the universe. To clarify matters in my mind I talked endlessly about it to Barbara, to a few Tongan friends on campus, to some academics here, and much later to my friend Tony Hooper, from the University of Auckland, who suggested that I turn the bit on "tuktuks" into an allegory presented in the style of ethnographic narratives. That suggestion set me on to one of the most enjoyable processes of writing I have experienced.

I first sounded out the idea of using the anus as a metaphor on my Tongan friends. They were highly amused, horrified, and disgusted. And when I said specifically that I was going to use it as a metaphor for love, beauty, and purity—that I was going to use it as a way of turning society upside down and inside out and giving it a thorough cleaning—they could not believe their ears. And when I floated the idea of a new philosophy of kissing the anus they roared and concluded that I was completely out of my mind. Maybe I was and maybe I still am, but I thoroughly enjoyed the experience, and wrote and wrote and talked on about it to my friends (some of whom started to avoid me) and wrote some more. Everyone here knew that I was writing a dirty book as everyone here knew that I had had a pain in the arse. They made the connection and came to the obvious conclusion. I had no more dignity left, so I went to town and made a thorough ass of myself dancing solo in the "middle of our zones of taboo." Oh, the life of a clown!

SUBRAMANI: *Did you have problems controlling the material at different stages—for example, tying everything to Bomboki's ailment? There are of course events which aren't directly linked to this kernel event.*

HAU'OFA: My main problem, and it shows in the book, arose from my tendency to include materials that are not directly relevant to the story. This includes insertion of certain details of village life in the Pacific, which, as a social analyst, I could not portray well in academic writing. They tend to slow down the story a bit. For example, on pages 15 to 18 I deliberately inserted a demonstration of greeting exchanges very common in the Pacific, reflecting the difficulty of maintaining privacy in very small and intimate communities. I also inserted commentaries on such things as the state of health services in the third world in general. And there is a big digression, almost a whole chapter in fact, when I brought in a completely imagined way of courting, that is, Oilei's courtship of Makarita. It sounded so ridiculous and original that I had to put it in. The exchanges of letters between Constable Butako and the New Zealand High Commission contain much extraneous material which I inserted because I wanted to reflect not only a wonderful way of Pacific letter writing but also the charming naïveté of many village people when they deal with outsiders who have power and money and may be placed in a quandary when they unexpectedly come face to face with apparent innocence. Diplomats and others like them have been trained to handle sophisticated matters and people; when out of the blue they are confronted, especially for the first time, with the unsophisticated, they get completely lost for words.

Part of the problem, I think, was that I had the tendency to allow my anthropological background to intrude into my fiction writing. Anyway, I was aware of the digressions but I decided to leave them in, tying them to the central story as best I could, for I believed that they would enrich the work. I might, of course, have been completely wrong.

SUBRAMANI: *When was the transplant episode conceived? I must admit that I felt uneasy with this portion of the novel. Isn't it exploiting the bizarre for its own sake? As if the novelist has heard the applause and readily takes encores.*

HAU'OFA: The transplant episode was conceived as an afterthought. I finished the first draft without it. But someone who read it said that the final part of the draft, the New Zealand episodes, was flat, straight, and not sufficiently crazy to be in line with the other parts. I agreed with him. Up to Oilei's journey to New Zealand, the episodes of his treatment get increasingly more bizarre. The New Zealand part of the draft was an anticlimax. I rewrote all of it with a view to making it more bizarre than the rest. Together with the final treatment at the Whakapohane Clinic, the anal transplant is the inevitable culmination of a series of increasingly bizarre events. Oilei has tried everything imaginable; the transplant is the natural next step.

Although I agree that it could have been put across differently, perhaps by toning it down, I remember that at the time I wanted to depict in the transplant, in a few brutal clear lines, the fundamental issues of racism and sexism by uniting in a single stroke black and white and male and female. And what better place for that unity to be forged than in the newly purified and glorified world of the anus?

Talking about lines and strokes reminds me of the fact that the main artistic influences in my writing have been the works of Australian political cartoonists of the late 1960s and early 1970s, men like Petty, Oliphant (who operated in the United States), Pickering, and especially Leunig. Their lines were extremely brutal, funny, sometimes poignant, and not infrequently crude. But their works throbbed with life and clarity. Another main influence was the American political cartoonist Walt Kelly. He was beautifully and ridiculously wordy, and also very funny and brutal. I'm almost certain that *Tales* was influenced by my fascination with Australian cartoonists, and my love of Walt Kelly's joyous verbosity might have had a bearing on *Kisses.*

When writing the transplant episode I knew that many sensitive souls would find it offensive. But with my early background close to the soil, and with the kind of company I'm partial to, I knew that it would appeal to a lot of others, especially to those with backgrounds similar to mine and to others with backgrounds in the ghettos of large cities. Chester Himes' stories about Harlem of the 1960s would have had a considerable following in the Pacific had his works been more accessible here. I thus wrote the episode knowing that it would offend some and appeal to others. And, as I have said, I also had a larger purpose for it. If the episode is seen as pandering to other things, then it is my misfortune and I'll have to live with it. If you survive the pain in the arse you can live with just about anything.

SUBRAMANI: *Evidently you have thought about language a great deal because there are references to different kinds of languages employed in fiction writing, for example, language of satire, allegory, apart from all the witticism and utopian dreaming. I want to ask if the profanities and obscenities are meant to reflect conversations in Pacific marketplaces and bars, for instance, or folk humour in general? Or is it something that you have invented?*

HAU'OFA: In my lifetime I have spoken seven Pacific languages including English. Four of these are Melanesian, which contain relatively few profane and obscene expressions. Two western Polynesian languages,

Tongan and Fijian, are rich in such expressions. But the most opulent of all is English, which, probably because of its global distribution, is forever spawning the most lurid profanities and obscenities.

Now, pious appearances and protestations notwithstanding, Tongans and Fijians are enthusiastic users of swearwords. I don't know about other Polynesians, or Micronesians, or Indo-Fijians because I do not speak their languages. Tongans and Fijians can be very earthy in their sense of humour, which, for someone like me, is one of their most endearing qualities. They can express it without resorting to obscenities. But they can, and do, use the most violent and lurid words and strings of invective among themselves merely for the joy of flouting the rules of etiquette, or to endear themselves to each other by merciless ribbing. And God help your eardrums if you happen to be around when two fully grown western Polynesian ladies quarrel in public. That's when the most colourful and graphic obscenities are released full-throttle and with utmost venom. But this is rare—perhaps because people realise that if it happens, all the underwear would be hoisted up the masts to flutter like that array of national flags outside the UN Building in New York.

Most of the profanities and obscenities in *Kisses* have been lifted straight from drinking places in Australia in the late 1960s and early 1970s and from English-language books and films. I love movies of most kinds except the likes of teenage and horror films. And I go most to see movies that make the least demand on one's intellect. They are generally full of physical and verbal violence.

In writing *Kisses* I did not consciously resort to profanities and obscenities to reflect aspects of certain Pacific or any other cultures as such. But since most of human behaviour is culturally determined, my work must necessarily reflect my very mixed background. I consider myself in part as a humorist, and in *Tales* I worked very hard and consciously on subtle and urbane humour. There is very little explicit obscenity in that book. However, because in *Kisses* I was writing on that section of the body that inspires so much crudity in language, I grasped the opportunity to indulge in undiluted earthy humour. I am by nature playful, and playing with words, obscene or otherwise, is an aspect of that nature. But this is only one aspect of my use of dirty language. I used it also for other purposes. Firstly, as I have already said, I resorted to it as a way of presenting the effect of physical agony on Oilei's psyche and on his relationship with those around him. But most important I used it as a most unlikely tool for a discourse on love, purity, and harmony. It's never been done or even thought of before, and that was part of the excitement. I knew that the idea was absurd. But since I adore absurdity, I said to myself, why not? Why not, indeed. So I started asking questions that I found very amusing because they were, or appeared to be, so absurdly real and the answers so absurdly true. Why should we continue to be ashamed of some parts of the body and not others? Why should we continue to loathe references to our organs of procreation and elimination, and not to other organs? Such questions led to other questions about social and cultural institutions that I started to explore in the novel. But because many of the questions I asked are absurd and silly by most cultural standards, I could not help but laugh as I wrote. And I seriously said to myself that if we give our organs of procreation and elimination the same consideration that we give the other parts of our bodies, we would eventually eradicate most of the obscene expressions in language and therefore in thought. That should go a long way towards helping us to be more loving and caring of each other. Ex-heavyweight boxing champion Oilei's search for a cure for his physical ailment is also a quest for purifying himself of violence and obscenity in language. Having attained his goal he invites everyone to kiss his arse. It is a joyous statement of the end of hatred, and a declaration of love for all humankind. It sounds bizarre but I'm serious about it; perhaps my Tongan friends were right and I should be confined to a nuthouse.

SUBRAMANI: *There are authors who insist they are writers not thinkers. Your first discipline, anthropology, obviously allowed you to think about society, culture, human systems. There are two related questions here: first, would you care to comment on the intellectual, ideological (the philosophy of arse-kissing) content of the novel; second, staying in two disciplines must cause a feeling of schizophrenia if not anxiety. Or is it simply a matter of switching discourses?*

HAU'OFA: I'm essentially a peasant albeit a highly educated one. There has been for many years a tussle between the peasant and the scholar in me. And I'm more than glad that the former has the upper hand. I like to view things from the ground up, preferably from the perspective of Lowly Worm. In short I'm a peasant writer and a declining academic.

Now to the intellectual and ideological content of the novel. I touched on this earlier when I talked about how my thoughts on local and international solutions to Pacific problems are reflected closely by

Oilei's search for a cure for his pain. Let me add a few more thoughts. I have had a degree of familiarity with social science theories, but most of them are useless outside the halls of academia and some are positively dangerous. Not one of them has helped much to improve the conditions of the peasantry and the urban working classes of the third world. Private enterprise is increasingly rapacious in our wide-open economies. Politics and government are corrupt and progressively authoritarian. Religion is devoid of spirituality. Neotraditionalism of the Pacific Indigenous Way variety touted by westernised, urbanised elite groups is abysmally narrow-minded and has recently proved itself to be unconscionably racist. I'm hypocritical, corrupt, self-centred, and fraudulent. So it takes a thief to catch a thief. These are strong admissions of one's views of self and others. But they have helped to inform whatever intellectual and ideological content there is in my writing. They have also enabled me to maintain a sense of balance, an amused tolerance of our human frailties, a readiness to accept the humanity in all of us, and a sense of humour that is essential for a joyously happy and playful life. That's the kind of mixed-up personality that produces things like the "tuktuk" allegory and the mock philosophy of love and respect for the anus. The immediate inspiration for this particular philosophy came from the international peregrinations in 1985 of Guru Rajneesh and his rich followers. He was one of the great religious frauds of recent decades who entertained the world with their impossible and phony philosophies, making themselves rich on the gullibility of so many people. Babu Vivekanand, with his mission to save humanity, is also a deliberate parody of the shenanigans of fake gurus the world over. In fact Babu's philosophy, unlikely as it is, is much less absurd than many others that have come to us from the East.

I used Babu's philosophy to raise the issue of taboos in our lives. If we examine carefully our systems of unmentionable cultural prohibitions, we may be able to see the roots of our collective fears and phobias. We impose taboos on things that we dread and loathe—most of which are not in themselves objects for such intense feelings. Taboos screen our perceptions of reality and thus distort them out of all proportion. As the anus is the most unmentionable part of the body, it is an extremely apt symbol of irrational taboos. There is a fundamental difference between the anus and the arse: the former is part of nature, the latter a cultural distortion of nature. Since we cannot destroy nature without destroying ourselves, we merely consign aspects of it that we dread and loathe to the edges of our collective mind where they remain to haunt us into violence in deed and in language. The essence of Babu's philosophy is that we can improve our capacity to love if we rid our minds of irrational fears and loathing. *Kisses* is really about a process of purification; the whole story of Oilei's quest for physical and later spiritual cure builds up to the ultimate state of purity.

I think that I have partly answered the second part of your question. I have virtually ceased to be a professional academic anthropologist for I have not kept up with theoretical and other developments in the discipline for at least ten years. But the ethnographer in me is still there, and that can be seen in my two works of fiction. I believe that a writer who concerns himself or herself with "society, culture, and human systems," as you put it, must also necessarily be an ethnographer. He or she must be able to observe analytically the minutiae of actual behaviour and arrange them into connected social and cultural patterns. He or she should be able to see these patterns quickly, and this could come from long and painstaking practice. I don't pretend to have developed this ability, but I have had at least four years of concentrated practice as a trainee and professional observer/social analyst on the ground in Trinidad, Papua New Guinea, and Tonga. And I have since spent much lesser periods in other parts of the South Pacific. My major training periods as a social and cultural analyst were spent in remote rural villages. These helped to keep me intellectually and emotionally close to the ground.

In short, although I'm no longer a professional academic anthropologist, I'm still an ethnographer of sorts, and this does not clash much with me as a writer of fiction. Mostly the two complement each other. What does trouble me really is that my work commitments at this university, especially as head of department and member of numerous standing and ad hoc committees, have left me with little time and hardly any space in the brain to concentrate on writing. But this is a matter of organisation on my part. I'm fairly disorganised, but I'm trying to improve. Maybe I will one day. It's never too late, says the pessimist.

SUBRAMANI: *Naturally I regard the publication of* Kisses in the Nederends *an important event in Pacific Literature. It expresses a new kind of freedom for Pacific Literature, a liberation from a narrow-minded seriousness that typifies the early literature; and of course the novel is a great comic work in its own right. The Samoan writer Albert Wendt has humour too, but it is of a cold, melancholic variety directed at a particular reality, whereas your work reveals an exuberant comic spirit that is directed against all reality. Are you nervous that this freedom and exuberance may not last very long in view of the current authoritarian tendencies in Pacific societies?*

HAU'OFA: The current authoritarian tendencies in the Pacific could indeed suppress all kinds of freedom. We face authoritarianism not only in our political systems but also in our religions, our communities, and even in the ranks of our own intellectuals. Personally, I can't afford to be nervous about the possibility of the loss of my own freedom, for that would hamper me from writing the way I do. I'm not at all being brave; I just don't think of it. But since you have raised the issue, I think that although there are freedoms being suppressed at the moment, the human spirit always rises, even from the ashes. You cannot suppress it forever. In my own little way I have always tried to open doors and to test the waters. When I returned to Tonga in the mid-1970s I did this initially through direct public action. Others have since gone further and have demonstrated that the supposedly most monolithic society in the South Pacific is not at all as inflexible as it appears. In fact there is a flexibility in Tongan society that indicates greater freedoms in the future. The structure of Fiji society has a built-in flexibility that will in the long run defeat all attempts to rigidify it.

As for me, since I discovered that I have some ability for writing I have concentrated my mind on it. I'm using it not only for creativity but also for opening doors—simply by exercising the freedom to think and write in my own ways. And I have always stubbornly resisted pressure to conform to ideas and visions that I disagree with or have reason to doubt. Much, if not most, of this pressure comes from closest kin, friends, and former friends. In our small Pacific communities the struggle for certain kinds of freedom comes right down to the most personal and intimate level. It is therefore very difficult, for one is bound to lose the affection of relatives and friends. The feeling of isolation can be acute but it is the price one pays for freedom. Anyway, solitude is part and parcel of a writer's life. One must accept one's place on the periphery of mainstreams. It is hard but the alternative is to give in, which I can't because I have this belief that writing is one of the very few contributions I can give to society. It may well be rejected but that's life.

SUBRAMANI: *Do you have any suggestions about how the novel ought to be read, posture-wise, and where it should be kept (placed) after reading?*

HAU'OFA: I would read it as a book about love, purity, harmony, and unbounded joy. I don't know about how others should. And since the book ends in Oilei's flight home from New Zealand, it should be placed in the back pocket of every airline seat in the world, next to the sick bag as the ever helpful Barbara says. And since Oilei spends a day in an Auckland hotel before his final treatment, I suggest that it should also be placed in every hotel room on top of the Gideon Bible. That should make me rich and Penguin more so.

PART IV

Revisiting

OVERLEAF: *Noqu Kalou noqu vanua,* Josaia McNamara, 2006

Thy Kingdom Come

The Democratisation of Aristocratic Tonga

First I would like to draw attention to the title of this essay. The first part, Thy Kingdom Come, is not merely a pun on the only existing monarchy in our part of the world, nor is it just part of a publicity stunt. It refers to recent developments in Tonga that exemplify a historical tendency for oppressed or threatened populations to look to religion for liberation or salvation. A powerless community that confronts seemingly entrenched or immovable forces may resort to the supernatural and religiously sanctioned moral codes for the advancement of its cause. Examples abound but the mention of a few recent ones may suffice to make the point: Poland and the Catholic Church under Communism; Iran and the Ayatollah under the Shah; and the ongoing struggle in Algeria.

In Tonga the agitation for political change not only has the support of the major churches, but church leaders themselves are in the forefront of the movement. The aim of these clergy, and the majority of the movement supporters, is to firmly establish the New Testament codes as the guiding principles of public and political behaviour. Significantly, however, the movement is strongly interdenominational and is therefore ideologically pluralistic, which may act as a check against the kind of religious political fanaticism that has been seen in Iran, Pakistan, and closer to home in Fiji as exemplified by a powerful section of the Methodist Church. In Tonga also, one of the prominent personalities of the movement is a strong atheist critic of religious establishments who has nevertheless been working closely with religious leaders on matters of national interest. Among the movement's supporters are members of the non-Christian Baha'i faith. Although the movement is Christian in its orientation, reflecting the strength of that religion in Tonga and indeed in our islands region, it is pluralistic in its inclusiveness of religious and sectarian doctrinal diversity and purely secular humanistic viewpoints. This accommodation of even seemingly irreconcilable ideological differences is a hallmark of the democratic culture. I shall return to this point later.

Before proceeding, I want to make one general observation. When the control of social and economic forces in a society shifts from one section of the community that had traditionally monopolised it to another section, it is inevitable that the newly empowered unit will begin to assert itself by demanding a share of institutionalised authority commensurate with its strength. Conversely, when the ruling section of a community loses control of the productive and other social forces in the society, its ability to govern effectively for the well-being of the community weakens accordingly. In such a situation the ruling section generally acts and reacts in ways that intensify the challenge to its political legitimacy. In the end it will have to adapt to the changed and changing environment—either by agreeing to a new reallocation of rights to govern or by stiffening its resistance using whatever means it can still command. This, however, is resistance from an already shaken position.

The realignment of forces within Tongan society today closely reflects the pattern of political development I have just sketched. As I shall shortly try to demonstrate, the ruling aristocratic section of the community has declined. The commoner section, however, is gaining power, from which position of strength it is demanding a commensurate share of the right to decide matters that concern its interests and welfare—that is, the interests and welfare of ninety-nine percent of the population. Behind the calls that have resounded over the past few years—for accountability in public affairs and for more ethical behaviour on the part of Tonga's national leaders—are demands by the newly empowered for a restructuring of the institutional arrangements of the society.

The process of democratisation of Tonga's political culture, of which the decline of the aristocracy and the rise of the commoner class is part, can be traced to the period around the middle of the nineteenth century and events that culminated in the establishment of a centralised monarchy at the expense of a hitherto multicentred aristocracy. Centralised kingdoms were generally built on the ashes of independently powerful aristocracies, and nineteenth-century Tonga was no exception. The modern state of Tonga was built on conquest warfare in which one warlord, the first of the present line of monarchs, managed through battlefield victories and judiciously forged alliances to overcome all armed opposition and to bring all territorial chiefs of the archipelago under his authority. He devised a new order that centralised in his hands all powers of political control, and he exercised those powers through a newly established bureaucracy. This process was akin to the establishment of the centralised kingdoms that contributed in large part to the ultimate demise of feudalism in Europe. An excellent example is the reign of Louis XIV, who emasculated the French nobility by bringing them into direct dependence on his court. Britain under the Tudor monarchs, the nineteenth-century rise of the Prussian kingdom, and the unification of Germany, in their different ways, exemplify the process.

The centralisation of authority in the hands of the Tongan monarch was achieved by the emasculation and dispossession of the hitherto largely autonomous and multicentred aristocracy, depriving it of any real independent power, in contrast with the other two remaining functioning aristocracies in the Pacific Islands, namely Fiji and Samoa.

It is to the advantage of any monarchy, in its relations with the aristocracy, to play them off against the rest of the population and vice versa. Two examples illustrate this point, although the outcomes might not have been intended. Tonga's equivalent of National Day or Independence Day is Emancipation Day, the most important annual secular holiday in the national calendar. Emancipation Day, celebrated for many decades—perhaps more than a century now—commemorates the occasion in 1862 when commoners were liberated by their first king—not from the shackles of any alien colonial regime but from alleged enslavement by their very own aristocracy. They were liberated from themselves. Little did people know then, or consciously know even today, that they were released from one form of bondage only to be subjected to another, relatively benign, form of subordination. But the ploy worked. The propagation of the belief in the royally decreed liberation—through annual celebrations, music, and poetry and through the schools—has ensconced the monarchy firmly and centrally in the national psyche and in the national affection.

The second example has been the use of the aristocratic representation in parliament to support the government. As is generally known, the thirty or so nobles of the realm elect among themselves a number of representatives equal to the number of representatives of the rest of the population, who constitute more than ninety-nine percent of the total. The nobles' representatives almost always vote solidly with government ministers, against the people's representatives, outnumbering them on every occasion. As is also generally known, ministers of the crown are appointed from outside the parliament by the monarch, hold their tenure at his pleasure, and are therefore directly responsible only to him. Moreover, while they hold office cabinet ministers are legally nobles or aristocrats, even though they may be of commoner rank by birth. The result has been that, until very recently, people have directed their disaffection and frustration with this lopsided form of representation against the aristocracy and cabinet ministers rather than against the monarchical system that has spawned and sustained it. The two examples I have used indicate the extent to which the aristocracy has been weakened—it has been transformed from knighthood into pawnhood on the political chessboard.

The specific measures that weakened the aristocracy and led to its decline in terms of its independent power and relative autonomy, its social utility, and its political legitimacy were instituted by the Code of 1862, the Constitution of 1875, and certain laws based on it (Lātūkefu 1975), which by the way is one of the oldest written constitutions in the world. These same measures formed the firm basis for the later emergence of a democratic culture in the country—and hence the growing demand for political restructuring in the 1990s. They included a drastic reduction in the number of land-controlling territorial chiefs; the introduction of primogeniture for both succession to title and inheritance of landed property; the abolition of traditional compulsory tributes to chiefs; and the individualisation of the land tenure system. I shall take each of these in turn to show their impact on both the aristocracy and the commoner class.

The first relevant aspect of the new order was the drastic reduction in the number of land-controlling titled chiefs from at least a hundred to around thirty. This was a reduction by at least two-thirds; it might even have been by three-quarters.[1] Traditionally in Polynesia, as elsewhere, the material basis of chiefly power was the control of lands and the people living on them. Chiefly lines that lost territorial control slipped into insignificance, and most of them eventually disappeared. The reduction of the number of estate-holding Tongan chiefs led to the fall or disappearance of most titles and the numerical weakening of the aristocratic ranks. Since the middle of the twentieth century, when the population began to increase rapidly, the aristocratic proportion of the total population has been falling behind. Numbers alone do not necessarily indicate strength, but when numbers are combined with social and economic power they become significant indeed. In any human group there is always an optimum number below which the group cannot function effectively in relation to other groups, even when the dice are loaded in its favour.

From the late 1960s especially, with the rapid expansion in the public and private sectors, the numerical and other related disadvantages of the aristocracy began to tell. Apart from positions that could be filled through political appointments that favoured the aristocracy, most strategic posts in the public sector went to commoners—the only ones with the talent and training to occupy them. The same is true of the private sector.

Second, the constitutional provision relating to primogenital succession has deprived the aristocracy of the great qualities of field leadership that were historically associated with them. In the past, chiefs, especially high chiefs, were selected by their peers from among eligible contenders. Because they were expected to be the managers of production within their territories, to actually rule their people, and to defend them against external aggression, only the fit and able could succeed to titles and hold them. The first king personified those qualities in his long struggle to accede to power and mould a new nation. He did not become monarch by virtue of birth alone; he had to overcome his rivals by demonstrating to them that he was far stronger, more skilful, and wiser than they were. The primogenital succession initiated by him and ensconced in the constitution was designed to prevent the kinds of competition and rivalry for succession that had led to much violence in the past. He should have known—for he himself had gone through the gruelling process of the overthrown system. Ironically, however, the measure he instituted removed all tests of fitness for office. Competition is very important in that it weeds out the weak and the unsuitable and brings forth and enhances strength of character. It enlivens a group, keeping its members fit, experienced, and mentally alert.

Apart from birth order, the only other criterion for Tongan succession is a negative one: disqualification on the ground of imbecility. But as we all know, one can be a certified idiot in more than a thousand nonmedically proven ways. The exclusive criteria of birth order and imbecility weaken any kind of succession for they foreclose the selection of the most able. The removal of the competitive factor from accession to power within a ruling group makes people take things for granted and saps much of its verve and life, rendering it ill suited to effective command of any social field wherein competition reigns supreme. One of the strengths of the Samoan and Fijian aristocracies is that their leaders are selected from eligible contenders to titles—perhaps explaining in part why their chiefs have shown greater willingness than Tongan chiefs to submit themselves to the general electorate in their bid for parliamentary seats.

Third, the abolition of compulsory tribute to chiefs, in the forms of labour and produce, has further eroded the strength of the aristocracy. Since 1862, chiefs have been forbidden to demand labour or produce from the people living on their estates. The implications of this prohibition go far beyond the loss of their main sources of wealth and therefore much of their power. It effectively ended the pivotal roles chiefs played in society: the management of economic production within their territories. This measure, together with the individualisation of land rights, removed chiefs from direct participation in the wider economy.

The development of the monetised sector of the national economy from the late nineteenth century and through the first half of the twentieth century was an alien development controlled by a relatively small number of European planters and traders. However, most Tongans remained in the semisubsistence peasant sector, producing for their own consumption and selling their surpluses to traders for target income. Significantly, people went to foreigners for their economic needs, not to their chiefs. The aristocracy benefited from this arrangement, not through active participation in the management of production and distribution on their estates, but in receiving rents from leases on their lands and traditional tributes that Tongans still paid voluntarily as part of their felt traditional obligations and, with the passage of time, on a diminishing scale. With the increasing marginalisation of the peasant sector of the economy, the significance of traditional tributes declined markedly. A class of people who were once economic managers, and who controlled the societywide redistribution system, has been transformed by circumstances into a class of recipients who expect privileges without obligations as a matter of birthright. Such a transformation leaves the people ill prepared to act effectively in the hugely competitive world of an open free-market economy.

When the commercial sector of the economy was thrown open to native Tongans after World War II, in part because of the emigration of most Europeans and part-Europeans who had controlled it, and when that sector expanded from the late 1960s on, the commoners, seasoned with toil, education, and skills training, were the ones equipped to move into that sector to establish themselves. Fortunes varied; many fell by the wayside; but some have succeeded to become wealthier than most of the aristocracy. With a few exceptions, the wealthiest and most economically powerful Tongans today are commoners. The same dominance obtains in the fields of education, the trades, and the professions. The two most notable exceptions from the aristocratic economic inertia have been the present monarch and his brother, the former prime minister, who had for decades been running commercial production on their estates. Their example has not been emulated by the rest of the aristocracy, and their operations have not been spectacularly successful.

The new land tenure system that came with the new order simultaneously empowered a small group of high chiefs and rendered them impotent. Under the constitution all land in the kingdom belongs to the monarch. The entire country is then divided into estates, some of which belong to the monarch, some to his government, and the rest to the thirty-three or so noble titles. Estate-holding chiefs, now called nobles to distinguish them from other and lesser chiefs, are required by law to divide their domains into parcels allotted to their people as individual holdings. Those who have their holdings registered in their names with the appropriate ministry are assured of their tenure by the state, which also guarantees the transmission of their property to their eldest sons. By 1975, sixty percent of the land allotted had been so registered, and more parcels are being registered every year (Kingdom of Tonga 1975, 38). Of the remaining allotted land, individuals can claim long occupancy rights, and the state is known to have upheld some of these claims. Finally, primogenital inheritance forecloses the rights of chiefs to play any real and meaningful role in the transmission of land rights on their territories from one generation to the next. All this has contributed to the weakening of the power of the aristocracy over their own estates. The system has, on the other hand, strengthened the commoner class by offering them security of tenure in perpetuity. They work on their holdings for their own exclusive benefit—free from extortion by the aristocracy and free from the kinds of land disputes common to most other parts of the island world. Even the nominal tax on allotment holdings has been removed.

Another explanation for aristocratic aloofness from the wider field of economic production is now evident: they have not only lost their traditional rights to command and mobilise labour and resources, but the ultimate control of the disposition of land parcels on their estates lies not in their hands but in those of the state. In compensation for their loss of independent powers and of their traditional sources of wealth, the nobles receive monthly stipends from the state, binding them even more to the patron–

client relationship with the monarch. Given that honour and prestige are bestowed at the monarch's prerogative, the dependence of the aristocracy on royal favour and patronage is further intensified.

Tonga is unique among the indigenous societies of the Pacific Islands in that all land rights are held by individuals and not by kinship groups such as clans or lineages. This system has spawned a strong sense of individual private ownership of property and a degree of individualism and individual freedom greater than obtains among those who live in more communally oriented societies whose group solidarity is materially rooted in joint holding of land rights and landed property.

But Tonga's primogenital inheritance means that younger sons and all women have no inheritance rights to their fathers' lands, unless their fathers control more than one land allotment. Today this means that most Tongans have no inherited legal land rights or holdings, which further means that the growing number of landless Tongans constitutes the largest rural and urban proletarian class among the indigenous populations of our region. Except for those who work in the public sector, and most do not, these members of the new proletariat generally owe little or nothing to the aristocracy and royalty and are therefore generally free of most traditional obligations beyond those to their immediate family circles. They and many of the others depend to varying degrees on financial and other forms of material remittances from their relatives overseas, further enhancing their independence from local and traditional constraints. They are independent and generally poor, and I believe they rank among the strongest supporters of the prodemocracy movement. They stand to gain from any change that would give their class more power.

Before the establishment of the monarchy there existed titled chiefs of various grades above the level of the heads of the minimal kinship units. There were minor chiefly titles, and grades of higher territorial chiefs, who formed a chain of command from the top of the social pyramid down to the commoners. This closely graded hierarchy constituted intricately interwoven networks of kinship ties that helped unite the entire society. The dispossession of most chiefly titles and their subsequent fall or disappearance from the political and important social arenas severed most of these links, further isolating the high chiefs from the population at large. In short, the strength of the kinship bonds that had traditionally united Tongan society from the top strata to the bottom has been weakening with each passing generation. Here again is another contrast between the Tongan aristocracy and those of Fiji and Samoa, where there are as many traditional leaders as there are landholding and other territorial units. In these societies, graded titles still connect the grass roots to the paramount chieftainships through blood as well as other ties.

In the past, the aristocracy monopolised the entire field of cultural and technical knowledge then available in the country. Commoners were referred to, as they still are sometimes, as *me'a vale,* "the ignorant." This was literally true; the rank and file of the lowest class were kept in the dark because knowledge was power and those who had it and strictly guarded it wielded power over others. Then came the Christian missionaries whose aim was to save everyone's soul. The new education system they introduced was made available to everyone for their own individual salvation. The new knowledge and training in new skills were sought after more than eagerly by Tongan commoners, leaving the aristocracy to nurse the kinds of knowledge that were becoming increasingly irrelevant for the conduct of everyday affairs in the changing socioeconomic environment. This voracious appetite for knowledge remains today and has earned Tongans a reputation among their fellow Islanders. The universalisation of knowledge and learning broke one of the main strangleholds that the aristocracy had over the people. In the past three decades in particular, ordinary Tongans in rapidly increasing numbers have received higher-level educations and have acquired a greater awareness of the world and their potential to excel, as well as a growing confidence in their ability and their new place in an evolving society.

Most of them have received their education overseas, where they have formed important links with individuals and institutions that may be activated for their advantage or that of the causes they espouse. Many of them are now residents of the democratic societies of the United States, Australia, and New Zealand, and an increasing number are resident in other Pacific Islands, employed by regional and international agencies or by transnational firms. From their bases abroad they are exerting significant influence on their homeland. For example, weekly or monthly publications by expatriate Tongans based in New Zealand, Australia, and the United States frequently discuss and editorialise upon national issues such as the prodemocracy movement. Every edition is airfreighted for distribution in the home country, supplementing a multiplicity of lively and fearless weeklies and monthlies published within Tonga and distributed widely internally and externally to the migrant communities. Furthermore, the use of sophisticated communications systems makes for instant international flows of information, connecting Tongans wherever they are located. National issues are internationalised through transnational networks of a highly mobile population, making it difficult for the powers that be to keep track of, let alone contain, any social movement with tentacles spread across the globe.

Within the country itself is a unique tertiary educational institution, the 'Atenisi Institute, that has processed generations of young Tongans in the ancient Greek philosophical traditions of dialogue and analysis. Its founder and director is Futa Helu, a former student of the great libertarian philosopher, the late John Anderson, professor of philosophy at the University of Sydney. 'Atenisi, an autonomous grassroots institution run on a shoestring budget, has succeeded, where those who have tried to establish the Marxist discourse elsewhere in our region have failed, in continuing to submit an entire society and its institutions to constant microscopic intellectual scrutiny. The effects on established social, political, and religious pretensions have been devastating. 'Atenisi has contributed immeasurably to the democratisation of Tongan society. Forcing people with backgrounds such as I have just outlined to remain in the ascribed subordinate place into which they were born, as some people have tried to do, is indulging in self-delusion, because that is another place, another time.

The relationship between commoner Tongans and their churches goes far beyond the field of education. The patron–client relationship between the monarchy and the aristocracy made it necessary for the high chiefs to move away from their communities into the capital to be close to the monarch, the source of power and patronage. In their absence, the leadership vacuum was filled by the only organisations that had intimate contact with the people—the churches—through their priests and pastors. Although access to the political and administrative hierarchies of the state was confined to royalty and their client aristocracy, the churches, through their hierarchies of clergy, schools, and other organisations, provided the initial opportunities for trained and ambitious commoners to rise and improve their status. More recently the state has been compelled to open up to commoners, but the earlier relationships between the churches and talented people remain strong. At the grassroots level, the churches have long replaced the aristocracy as the most significant influence on the daily life of the people. As the people become increasingly better educated and more democratic minded, so have the leaders of their churches.

The central authorities are fully aware of the special bond between the two groups. In late 1992, in preparation for the early February 1993 general elections, the monarch summoned the church leaders for an audience during which he requested their active cooperation in the formation of a political party to counter the prodemocracy movement. It is indicative of the standing of the aristocracy that the monarch did not try to recruit their assistance. Their efforts would have been futile. However, church leaders made no move to comply with their monarch's request. At the general elections, the prodemocracy candidates for the main island, which makes up two-thirds of the national population, swept all the seats with large majorities, scoring their biggest polling-station victories in those villages most closely associated with the royal family and the biggest of the big chiefs. They captured all the villages of Tongatapu except one or two.

These events show that the deliberate emasculation of the aristocracy—and its manipulation to bolster the monarchical authority—have in the long run rendered the monarchy vulnerable by exposing it directly to the grass roots. In the ideal situation an absolute monarchy should have a relatively strong aristocracy to act as a buffer against the general population. But the weakened Tongan aristocracy is unable to offer such a buffer now that it is needed. There is therefore a rising and direct popular demand for the monarch to relinquish his political powers and accept the status of the British and Scandinavian monarchs—to reign but not to rule. Such a demand was inconceivable only five years ago in 1988, but events have moved faster than most observers would have anticipated.

In the three remaining truly aristocratic societies of the South Pacific (Tonga, Fiji, and Samoa), Tongan chiefs have the least control of and influence on the daily life of their people. The only area where the aristocracy exerts any meaningful control at all is at the apex of the state structure: in Parliament, the Cabinet, the Privy Council, and to a diminishing degree the bureaucracy, through royal patronage. This is their last remaining bastion of power. Their resistance against democracy is thus explained and is entirely human: no one relinquishes their main sources of livelihood and power willingly.

Most of the factors that have contributed to the structural weakening of the aristocracy have also contributed to the growing independence, democratisation, and empowerment of the commoner class. Tonga's progressive absorption into the world economic and cultural system has supplied the means for the rise of the ordinary people. These means are rooted in the international system, and no tiny, local, endogamous group anywhere can command them by the mere fiat of constitutionally sanctioned right of birth. They can only be mastered by talent, training, and performance in the open, competitive marketplace. Here the commoner class of Tonga has its greatest advantage. Constituting ninety-nine percent of the population, this class, by virtue of sheer numerical supremacy, commands the pool of talent needed for a modernising society to develop and operate within an extremely complex international system. From this pool has come the call for a renewed national covenant. The call has come from the ranks of those on whom the country depends for its social, economic, and spiritual advancement, from the ranks of those who actually hold the strength of the nation.

Tongan society today has a vibrant, democratic culture whose characteristics include an educated and increasingly informed population that exercises individual freedom of expression and association; a predominance of private and individual ownership of property used in a free-market economy; an increasingly open system that allows for social mobility based on individual achievement; a mobile internationalised middle class that provides among other things intellectual and ideological leadership to social movements; a grassroots leadership that is no longer fettered by ancient constraints; a population of a traditional lower class that is now re-formed into a new, open class structure economically independent of the traditional system of patronage; a lively free press through which national and other issues are debated openly, and even heatedly, and through which alleged misconduct in high places is exposed fearlessly; a rapidly growing belief in the necessity for a popular and responsible form of government; and an established ruling order that has thus far reacted in restrained ways to the rising challenge to its authority and has made hesitant and tentative moves to engage in a kind of dialogue alien to its nature.

Although Tonga has an absolute monarchical form of government, its population has developed a democratic culture to the extent that commensurate changes in the political institutions are but a matter of time because the walls of Jericho are already shaken.

In making these statements, I do not wish to write the aristocracy off—far from it. Like other indigenous institutions in the Pacific that have survived the trauma of drastic changes wrought by imperialism and neocolonialism over the last two hundred years, the Tongan aristocracy has shown a remarkable resilience. Despite its emasculation at the establishment of a new order in the nineteenth century, it still performs essential functions that have been associated with it for hundreds of years.

Like everything else, the aristocracy is changing, and there are signs of reinvigoration in its ranks. In general the current heirs to noble titles, together with their siblings, like other young people of their generation, are far better educated than their parental and grandparental generations. Like their peers in the commoner ranks, an increasing number of them are securing university qualifications and are earning their postings in the public sector through merit. A number of the younger generation are entering the private sector, sometimes in partnership with their commoner peers. With others in their generation, they have gone through the same rigour of training in the open marketplace of learning and have emerged tried and tested. They seem to be more egalitarian in their attitudes than their forebears and may even be more favourably disposed towards an open and democratic system than their elders have understandably been.

In closing, I would like to quote the concluding part of a speech I gave in Tonga in 1992 on the same topic. This extract expresses a sentiment that perhaps most Tongans feel about their society. Despite our differences and confrontations—and we are a disputatious people like everyone else—we have a profound loyalty to our common heritage and to our identity as a single people who have travelled together for perhaps two thousand years or more if New Zealand and American archaeologists are to be believed. We are all conscious that ours is a tiny community (of largish people nevertheless), and that we are at one of the crossroads of our history. At the present crossroad we have to find a route along which we will be able to continue seeding traces of memory for those who will come after us. We owe this to those who have gone before us, for the memory they have bequeathed. What follows may find echoes in some other communities in our region. I use the first personal pronouns because I am now talking to myself.

> Although the aristocracy will always be few in number, Tonga will continue to need from them far more than their social and economic contributions to our progress. Like their ancestors, they serve the nation in ways that no one else can; and therein I believe lies their great and continuing importance. They are the foci of our culture and our identity as a single people, as well as being the signposts of our historical continuity as a nation. Our remembered past is inextricably bound up with the rising and falling fortunes of our leading lineages. And so has been the case with our documented history from the turn of the nineteenth century. We have travelled together with our aristocracy for over a thousand years, and their leadership has given us reasons to

be proud of our history, our heritage, and ourselves as a nation. We will still travel together with them, albeit along new and uncharted routes towards the end of this century and into the next millennium.

We still expect to see in our aristocracy, as in no other group in our society, the ideal qualities of our collective personality. In our hurly-burly, free-for-all, dog-eat-dog modern society, we look to them for such qualities in social interaction as civility, graciousness, kindness, and that calming aura of a unifying presence in our midst. This may explain why we get very disappointed whenever they behave as mere mortals, exhibiting the follies and foibles that are the lot of humanity in general. Perhaps we have been expecting too much from them. Nevertheless, they are part of us as we are part of them, and have always been so. And although developments in the past decades have brought us into confrontation with some of them, we as Tongans have maintained a sense of profound respect and an abiding affection for them. They also feel the same for us, despite our differences. We have an expression, *'oku ou pahia 'ia koe,* "I am fed up with you," which we utter when we get exasperated with members of our own families. We never really mean it. That is why I have a certain degree of confidence that in the near future we will get together with our leaders and work out a new national consensus that will take us into the next century as a revitalised community and a stronger, even more united people.

Notes

This essay is a very slightly revised version of a Distinguished Lecture to the Association of Social Anthropologists in Oceania, at Kona, Hawai'i, in March 1993, and a 25th Anniversary Public Lecture at the University of the South Pacific, Suva, in April 1993. A published version first appeared in serial form in *The Weekender* (Suva: Media Resources) in 1993.

1. Gifford (1929, 132–144) provides a partial list of seventy-five chiefly titles. He mentions others elsewhere in the same book; even so, some titles are not mentioned at all.

References

Gifford, E. W. 1929. *Tongan Society. Bernice P. Bishop Museum Bulletin* 61. Honolulu: Bishop Museum.

Kingdom of Tonga. 1975. *Statistical Abstract.* Nuku'alofa: Statistics Department, Government of Tonga.
Lātūkefu, S. 1975. *The Tongan Constitution: A Brief History to Celebrate Its Centenary.* Nuku'alofa: Tonga Traditions Committee.

His Majesty King Tāufa'āhau Tupou IV

An Appreciation

IMMEDIATELY AFTER the passing away of someone we love, we recall and talk only of the good things he or she has done with and for us. The human failings of the loved one are shelved for later occasions. Earlier today, far away from where we are, our beloved and revered Father of the Nation was launched on his voyage to another realm. We wish that we were at home for that final farewell.[1] I will touch only on how and why we came to hold him so dearly in our hearts. This is neither the time nor the place for saying anything else.

There is little doubt that throughout all the turmoil of the last two or so years, what kept our country together was the reverence and affection that we had for our king. When Tāufa'āhau Tupou IV acceded to the throne some forty years ago he was much respected, but had yet to capture the hearts of the public at large. Only those who were closely associated with him, in government and among the church leadership, saw the very humane side of him and responded accordingly. Besides, his immediate predecessor, the universally popular and beloved Queen Sālote, was still the focus of the national affection. Hers was a hard act to follow. She was an immensely warm person and was very close to her people. Because she acted very much the true constitutional monarch, leaving the governance of the kingdom to the cabinet, and was largely free from the burden of the state, she was able to direct her energy to her interest in culture and her personal concern for her people. She is said to have had a network of women in villages throughout the kingdom, who reported to her on the happenings in their communities, and she responded with compassion, and helped those who were in need. She knew every family in the country. Her palace was the gathering place of leaders of traditional culture, and being a poet and songwriter herself, she always filled her court with musicians and performers. She was so loved that people went every day to the palace to present the best produce from their farms, the best mats and tapa they had crafted, and the best catches from the reefs. This enabled her to maintain her crowded court and help those in need. As she had lived through two world wars and the Great Depression of the 1930s, she was very much aware of the untold suffering these events had visited upon the world and she strove for the rest of her life to shield her people from international influences.

Meanwhile her eldest son and heir apparent, Crown Prince Tungī, was occupying himself in the opposite direction. As the first, and for many years the only, Tongan with a university degree, he understood as no one else in the country could the necessity for the kingdom to change in accommodation to the demands of the times. It was not possible to be isolated from international influences. The major disastrous events of the first half of the twentieth century affected the island kingdom as they affected the rest of the world. Thus, when he took up the reins of government as prime minister in 1949, he set out to drag the country into the twentieth century while maintaining its existing political and cultural institutions. His mother, still reigning monarch, was taking care of the cultural institutions; the rest was his responsibility.

My late aunt, Nānisi Helu, with whose family I lived for several years, was a member of Queen Sālote's small circle of night companions. Early every evening she would leave home to spend the night with the queen, often talking into the late hours. She told me that one night while they were thus occupied, the queen called out to her son, who was working late in the adjacent room. "E Tungī," she said, "why don't you start a business and build something for the security of your children?" After a pregnant pause, Tungī replied rather formally, "Your Majesty, my business is the welfare, security, and happiness of our people. Their well-being will be the security of our family." And he lived up to that demanding charge for the rest of his life. There was no other objective. He never tried to enrich himself personally. Every venture that he started, successfully or otherwise, was all for his people.

The ministers he had chosen in the 1950s and the early 1960s, and who served him for decades thereafter, followed his example. They had the privileges and perks of high office, but not one of them engaged personally in business while in office. And when they retired, they were too old and spent to start any new businesses with resounding success. This generation of ministers included Prince Tu'ipelehake (the king's younger brother), Baron Vaea, Baron Tuita, Ve'ehala, 'Akau'ola, Dr. Sione Tapa, Dr. Langi Kavaliku, and Mahe'uli'uli Tupouniua. I know one of them who had received offers of lucrative posts overseas in the 1970s and 1980s but declined because of his loyalty to the king. Tupouniua was seconded with the king's blessing to be the first director-general of what is now the Pacific Islands Forum Secretariat. These men held their high offices for thirty or more years, not because their tenure was dependent only on His Majesty's pleasure and favour, but because they were imbued with their leader's ideals, vision, and selfless service and had developed enduring loyalty and affection for him. They gave him the best years of their lives, as their compatriots of another era had presented Queen Sālote with the best produce and products of their labours.

As for the vast majority, the ordinary people of Tonga, their affection for their monarch took more time to grow as they came to know him more slowly. He was a man of few words, and publicly he spoke with such a soft voice that one had to turn up one's ears to hear him, even when he spoke through a microphone. It was worse in the 1950s when there were no microphones. On most occasions when he appeared informally in public he said nothing, and on traditional formal occasions his orators spoke for him. But he appeared so frequently that his mere presence and mana, and the fact that he had given up his time to be among us, spoke eloquently to our hearts, as only the voice of silence can.

He lived a very simple life. The royal palace is an old rambling nineteenth-century mansion, little modernised and sparingly furnished. His alternative residence on the windward coast of Tongatapu was constructed in simple and elegant traditional design, with roofs resembling the upturned hulls of oceangoing canoes. From the late 1980s on, he survived on a simple weight-controlling diet and exercises including cycling, rowing, and working out with weights. He persuaded his people to do likewise, and the population began walking slightly faster than Tu'imalila, the Galapagos tortoise that Captain Cook gave them in the 1770s, and who lived well into the 1960s. Tupou Fā had neither the time nor the inclination for true luxury. As a result he did not care to develop a taste for fashion, and often donned some wonderfully weird outfits.

Much of his spare time was dedicated to his passion for reading and experimental animal husbandry. He read books and magazines on a wide range of world affairs, and often surprised visiting foreign dignitaries with his well-informed knowledge of current affairs and developments in scientific research and so forth. A special interest was in reading on the historical origin of Polynesia, and he tried to understand the Malay languages of Southeast Asia for he believed that our ancestors originated in that region.

One day he told me that the Polynesian word for chiefs derived from the Malay Indonesian word for men who stayed up all night to see that their voyaging vessels were safely on course. The trouble with our chiefs nowadays, he added, is that they start sleeping well before dusk and wake up long after dawn when everyone else has gone to work.

His Majesty also turned the palace grounds—which once had reverberated with the sound of beautiful melodies and poetry and with the sight of performers dancing the night away—into a zoological garden for experimental breeding of such feathered friends as geese, Peking ducks, and doves. He only had to step outside the palace to be in his open-air laboratory. And as usual, his underlying object was the well-being of his people, providing them with opportunities to raise such fowl on their farms as cheap additional sources of protein and as healthier alternatives to mutton flaps and other life-shortening foods. The king also informed his people through a radio broadcast that geese were excellent guards of people's homes. The big birds honk very loudly when strangers approach and will attack them if they enter the birds' home territory. It was the geese, he said, that once saved Imperial Rome when barbarians were sneaking towards the city under cover of dark.

But there was a problem. The geese that the king brought did not themselves hatch their eggs. This was done in specially warmed incubators that had to be maintained at a certain temperature: if too hot the eggs would fry. Most village farmers could not afford the necessary equipment. When I left Tonga in 1983, His Majesty was still raising his geese; perhaps as a form of relaxation. I found it very moving when I looked out through the windows of the Palace Office one day and saw him sitting under a big tree contemplating his garden of birds.

On the few occasions when I had to see him, he was always courteous and fatherly. In his presence, I could feel his mother in him and imagine those of his illustrious lineage who had served our nation from time immemorial. As Tongans we believe in the three pillars of our society: *koe lotu, koe pule'anga fakatu'i, moe fonua* (the Christian church, the monarchy, and the nation). This image underpins what I shall say now and I ask you to keep it in mind.

When Tupou Fā was still a small boy, the queen his mother sent him to school—not to the government Tonga College, which was the training institution for the civil service, but to Tupou College, the Wesleyan Methodist Church's boys' school. The college staff was instructed to treat him like any other student. There the young prince experienced intimately the life conditions of ordinary Tongans. More important, he formed enduring relationships with many of the boys and young men who would become leading clergymen and lay churchmen. In later years, after his return from the University of Sydney, he rekindled these old schoolboy ties with the leadership of the largest and most powerful church in the land. He maintained his ties with Tupou College and became the regular guest of honour at the Tupou College annual prizegiving and speech night, throughout the 1950s at least. I was at the school in the early 1950s and regularly shook his hand for prizes in good behaviour, religious knowledge, and one or two others.

He was a deeply religious man; he was a lay preacher and on his accession he assumed the formal headship of the Wesleyan Church. Through his active involvement in the religious life of the community, he strengthened one of those three pillars of society and gathered to himself the loyalty of religious leaders and their equally religious congregations.

As regards the second pillar of society, the government, Crown Prince Tungī, first as holder of several portfolios, including education, and later as prime minister, established the social and economic infrastructure that enabled Tongan commoners to aspire to opportunities, positions, and personal liberties that were hitherto denied to them. As minister of education he opened up the overseas scholarship award system by having it based on merit. Hitherto scholarships for secondary schools in New Zealand and Australia were only for the children of the nobility.

When Tāufa'āhau (to use the late king's birth name) entered university and successfully completed his arts law degree, no Tongan, not even anyone of noble rank, was allowed to receive a university-level education. The nature of social stratification was such that no one could be the equal of the crown prince. A popular saying in the 1950s was *'Oua e fakatatau kia Tāufa'āhau* (do not try to be the equal of Tāufa'āhau).

But after his return from Sydney the crown prince applied his traditional rank, state authority, and the mana of the most highly educated man in the country to the pushing through of his modernisation of Tonga and the opening up of a closed society. He would eventually open up everything except the very top strata of the decision-making authority and the traditional ranking order. He saw that the modernisation of the country would succeed only if the population were educated and trained in the skills that modernisation requires. He established the Tonga High School, the first senior secondary school in the country, and opened it to commoners. When he ascended the throne, scholarships to tertiary institutions abroad were increased in number and distributed on the basis of merit. The expanded bureaucracy and the newly established statutory bodies were manned largely by educated commoners, who rose to the top in these organisations as well as in the headship of the civil service departments.

The opening up of the scholarships abroad and their expansion in the 1970s, the rising number of senior secondary schools within the country, and the rise of other tertiary institutions (including the USP Centre, now USP Tonga campus) were, I believe, the most important development in Tonga in the second half of the twentieth century. People attributed this to the monarch. It was the achievement that launched his entry into the hearts of his people. Other infrastructural components took time to have an impact, and a number of these spluttered along, as they still do today. But educational opportunities have an immediate and direct impact on individuals and their families. They are the keys that open up the world for people. To understand why the king's educational policies so endeared him to the people, we must appreciate the singular importance of education to the commoners of the kingdom. Tongans have been obsessed with education for about a century and a half. It is the most important thing for every parent. For commoner families, education for their sons and daughters was the only way for them to overcome the enormous barriers erected to keep them in their lowly places. The traditional word for commoners is *kau me'a vale* (the ignorant ones). The first king of modern Tonga, Tupou I, was struck by a verse in the Bible that says "My people are destroyed through lack of knowledge" (Hosea 4:6). He encouraged the missionaries to establish real schools. Tupou College was born one hundred and forty years ago. Since then the "ignorant classes"—the vast majority of Tongans—have struggled, through education, to surmount their ascribed conditions.

Of all the Tongan songs I know, only one popular song is about His Late Majesty. In English translation it is called "The Stranger in Jerusalem." It is a song of praise and rejoicing. It says nothing about his lineage or his achievements in the development of his country; it is all about his educational achievement at Sydney University. It is an extravagant encomium and a jubilant and rousing song that we sing with gusto, basking in his reflected glory. But he has opened the way for us to be educated at universities, too, and even to take degrees that are higher than his.

The infrastructure that the king built, in the areas of transport, communications, finance, and so on, contributed to the emergence of a commoner entrepreneurial class that has become wealthy and influential; it is from this class that the first commoner prime minister, Dr. Feleti Sevele, has been selected.

The two decades from the late 1960s were the most exciting years of the transformation of Tonga into a modern society. But these developments have naturally led our people to demand changes in the apex of power and authority, as the final stage of our transformation. Though natural, it is an unforeseen outcome of the forces that His Late Majesty unleashed. We owe the possibilities to him.

The last pillar of our society is the nation: the people. I have touched on this throughout what I have had to say, because in reality we cannot compartmentalise life. I will give two concrete examples to illustrate what I have said about his keeping in touch with ordinary people.

As a former star athlete, rugby player, and rower, at home and in Sydney, he developed an abiding interest in sports, especially team sports. He frequented rugby matches, and his presence at test matches between Tonga, Fiji, and Samoa galvanised his national team into overcoming the opposition or into losing honourably. He introduced soccer and netball, which are far from being as popular as rugby. And it was always touching to pass a soccer or a netball match on the field by the palace and see him sitting there as the sole spectator. But the soccer players played as if the entire population were there. Indeed, the whole population *was* there: Tupou Fā was Tonga.

Secondly, while he was physically able, he attended every annual agricultural show in every district of the kingdom, even in the remote northern Niuas. His presence at these shows was eagerly anticipated. As he passed along the stalls you could see the happiness, the affection, the pride, in the faces of small struggling farmers. These are two examples of the ways in which Tupou IV related to his people. He was not only their king; he was their caring father.

Although Tonga is known for its hereditary rank system, relationships between the ranks are based not only on command but also on the blood ties that link us to those above us. Theoretically, we can all trace our genealogies right up to the royal family. Those above us are not only our overlords but also our senior relatives. Unfortunately, many of them have used their rank primarily to command us and suppress our aspirations. But Tupou IV chose to use the principles underlying relationships based on blood. He would use his authority to command when it was necessary to push through his modernisation programme against opposition from his advisers or to protect the monarchic structure of the nation. Rightly or wrongly, he firmly believed that the House of Tupou is necessary for preserving Tonga's centuries-old identity and independence, and for the freedom to develop the country in its own ways.

Under his rule the nation reemerged as a changed family, with him as its benevolent paterfamilias, the Father of the Nation. Metaphorically, we can say that our nation is a body through the vessels of which flows the blood that feeds every part and keeps the whole alive. At the centre is the heart that pumps the life-giving blood through the nation, recirculating it continuously as it delivers the nutrients and carts away the waste. The House of Tupou is the heart of Tonga.

For the past forty years Tupou Fā has been the head and the heart of our national family; he has been both the benevolent father who led and guided us and the mother who nurtured and loved us. We love him, we honour him, in grief we mourn his passing. The sun has taken shelter in the temple of the nation, the land is shrouded in sorrow, the dawn of a new day is coming upon us. In love we embrace the Sun of Yesterday, we shall keep him warm in the temple. With hope we hail the Dawn of Tomorrow. God defend the House of Tupou, God bless our nation.

Tu'a 'ofa atu.

Note

1. This eulogy was delivered at the Ecumenical and Memorial and Thanksgiving Service for the late king of Tonga, His Majesty Tāufa'āhau Tupou IV, held at Holy Trinity Cathedral, Suva, Fiji, 19 September 2006.

Blood in the Kava Bowl

In the twilight we sit
drinking kava from the bowl between us.
Who we are we know and need not say
for the soul we share came from Vaihi.
Across the bowl we nod our understanding of the line
that is also our cord brought by Tangaloa from above,
and the professor does not know.
He sees the line but not the cord
for he drinks the kava not tasting its blood.
And the kava has risen, my friend,
drink, and smile the grace of our fathers
at him who says we are oppressed
by you, by me, but it's twilight in Vaihi
and his vision is clouded.

The kava has risen again, dear friend,
take this cup . . .
Ah, yes, that matter of oppression—
from Vaihi it begot in us unspoken knowledge
of our soul and our bondage.
You and I hold the love of that inner mountain
shrouded in mist and spouting ashes spread
by the winds from Ono-i-Lau,
Lakemba, and Lomaloma
over the soils of our land, shaping
those slender kahokaho and kaumeile
we offer in first-fruits to our Hau.
And the kava trees of Tonga grow well,
our foreheads on the royal toes!
The Hau is healthy,
our land's in fine, fat shape for another season.

The professor still talks
of oppression that we both know,
yet he tastes not the blood in the kava
mixed with dry waters that rose to Tangaloa
who gave us the cup from which we drink
the soul and the tears of our land.
Nor has he heard of our brothers who slayed Takalaua
and fled to Niue, Manono, and Futuna
to be caught in Uvea by the tyrant's son
and brought home under the aegis of the priest of Maui
to decorate the royal congregation and to chew for the king
the kava mixed with blood from their mouths,
the mouths of all oppressed Tongans,
in expiation to Hikule'o the inner mountain
with an echo others cannot hear.

And the mountain spouts ancestral ashes
spread by the winds from Ono-i-Lau, Lakemba, and Lomaloma
over the soils of our land, raising fine yams,
symbols of our manhood, of the strength of our nation,
in first-fruits we offer to our Hau.
The mountain also crushes our people,
their blood flowing into the royal ring
for the health of the Victor and of Tonga;
the red waters from the warm springs of Pulotu
only you and I can taste, and live
in ancient understanding begat by Maui in Vaihi.

The kava has risen, my brother,
drink this cup of the soul and the sweat of our people,
and pass me three more mushrooms which grew in Mururoa
on the shit of the cows Captain Cook brought
from the Kings of England and France!

Notes

This poem was originally published in *Mana Review* 1(2) (1976):21–22.

Tangaloa and Maui are well-known Polynesian gods, and Vaihi (Hawaiki) is the legendary ancestral homeland. The *kahokaho* and the *kaumeile* were long yams sent as first-fruit tributes to the Tu'i Tonga, the semidivine ruler. (Orators refer to the monarch as the "Hau.") Takalaua, the twenty-third Tu'i Tonga, was killed by two men, whom his son caught, took to a special kava ceremony, forced to chew the dry roots of the kava plant for the king's kava bowl, and then had butchered for distribution to the assembled chiefs of the realm. Pulotu, the paradise, was presided over by Hikule'o, the goddess of fertility, whose earthly representative, the Tu'i Tonga, received (on her behalf) the annual first-fruit tribute. To Pulotu (and hence to Hikule'o) went the souls of dead chiefs, and from Pulotu came the great long yams—the sons of Tonga.

Index

Aborigines, 4, 50, 73, 75, 106
aesthetics, xvi, 82, 85–86, 89
Alo, Allan, 91
American Samoa. *See* Western Samoa
Anderson, John, 166
anthropology: creative writing contrasted with, 107–108, 146, 148–149, 151; Hau'ofa's training in, x–xi; and history, 61–62, 64, 68; in Oceania's universities, 44; and Pacific Islanders, 3–10, 101, 104, 107–108. *See also* ethnography
Aotearoa, 33, 35. *See also* Maori people; New Zealand
'Atenisi Institute, xvi–xvii, 166
Australia: aid, development, and migration, 15–22, 36, 41, 50, 165; influencing Oceania's educational systems, 14, 91, 176; as regional center, xii, 11, 12, 32, 44, 45; in South Pacific Forum, 47–49
authoritarianism, 150, 152
autonomy: cultural, 61, 63, 80; individual, 29, 63; national and regional, 21, 29–30, 38, 61, 81, 92; Tongan, 160

Banaba, 46
Beier, Georgina, xvi–xvii, 83, 89
Beier, Ulli, xvi–xvii, 83, 89
belittlement, xiv–xv, xvi, xix, 28–39, 42, 46
Bikini Atoll, 46
Bishop Museum, 8
Butafa, Frederick: *On the Reef* (painting), 95; *The Voyage* (painting), 25

Canberra school of Pacific historians, 61–62
Christianity: effects of, 23, 28, 47, 63, 75, 106; in Hau'ofa's youth, 99–100; as Tongan societal pillar, 175. *See also* missionaries
class: commoner, 158, 160; emergent structures of, xii, 13, 22–23, 44, 69; middle, 96–97; ruling, affluent, and privileged, xii, 13–15, 18, 20–23, 36, 61, 70; working, 44, 150. *See also* elites; peasants and peasantry; poor people
colonialism, xiv, 3, 18, 46–47, 75, 106. *See also* neocolonialism
connectedness, xv, xx, 30, 32–39, 54–58, 81, 92–93
Cook Islands, 11, 14, 15, 33, 60, 77n.2, 81
Cousins, 65
creativity, 56, 80, 84–89, 103, 141–142, 152

Davis, Sir Thomas, 60
decolonisation, 11, 19–22, 43, 47–48, 56
democratisation of Tonga, 157–171
dependency: and interdependency, 36, 41; in Melanesia, 29; in Pacific region, 27, 29–30, 38–39, 47, 91, 106; theory of, xiii; in third world, 34. *See also* regional integration
development: anthropology associated with, 8; critiqued, xii–xiii; international promotion of, 38, 42, 47, 54, 66, 70–71; regional, 11–23, 47, 50, 76; sustainable, 37–38
diaspora, xv–xvi, 12–14, 57, 92. *See also* population migration and movement

Earle, Sylvia, 52, 59
education: curriculum, 15, 42–44, 70–71, 76, 81, 87; regional system of, 14–15, 37, 42–44; in Tonga, 165–166, 176–177. *See also* University of Papua New Guinea; University of the South Pacific
elites, 11–23, 61, 70, 98, 106–107, 150. *See also* class, ruling, affluent, and privileged
English language, 5, 6, 8, 32, 67, 148, 177; Hau'ofa's use of, x, 147; as Pacific language, 13, 14, 71
environment, 72, 91; global, 37, 55, 87; threats to Oceania's, 29, 49–50, 67, 87, 103
ethnography: and history, 61, 64, 68; as writing style, x, xi, 6, 103, 108, 145, 151

Federated States of Micronesia, 37
fieldwork, xi, 3, 4, 7, 8–9, 151
Fiji: coups, ix–x, 44, 82; economy, 15, 33, 35, 39n.1; educational system of, 14, 15; as part of Polynesia, 39n.1; political structure of, 33, 152, 159, 161, 165, 167; population characteristics, 16, 50, 74, 81. *See also* Fijian people; Fiji Indian people
Fijian people: aristocracy, 33, 161; defined, 50; fishing and land rights of, 54; humour of, 140–141; land, relationship with, 74–75; language of, 66–67, 71, 74, 148; migration by, 15–16, 35; music of, 91; sense of time, 66–67. *See also* Fiji Indian people
Fiji Indian people, 14, 15, 35, 50, 148
Fortes, Meyer, 9
Freeman, Derek, 7–8, 10
French language, 14, 71
French Polynesia, 11, 33, 37, 50, 77n.2
Futuna, 33, 77n.2

genealogies, 66, 72, 178
global economy and markets, xii, xiii, 31, 42, 69, 70–72, 80
globalisation: and capitalist development, xiii, 144; contrasted with Pacific cultural practices, xix–xx, 42, 69–71, 76, 80–81; in Hau'ofa's life, x; resisted by the Oceania Centre for Culture and the Arts, 88–89. *See also* global economy and markets; global system
global system, 36, 61, 71, 88
Grace, Patricia, 65

Hawai'i, 30, 33, 34, 35, 38, 62, 81. *See also* Hawaiian people
Hawaiian people, 50, 66, 70, 72

Hawke, Bob, 18–19
Helu, Futa, xvi–xvii, 73, 166
Helu, Nānisi, 173
Himes, Chester, 99, 147
history: and anthropology, 4, 61, 64, 68; Canberra school of Pacific, 61–62; education, 43–44, 80; in genealogies, 66; identity associated with, 46–47; in landscapes and seascapes, 53–58, 66, 72–77; Pacific historiography, 63–77, 80–81; and prehistory, 62–64; spiral of, 69–72; temporal divisions in, 28, 62–63, 64, 66–68; in Tonga, 169–170. *See also* oral narratives and tradition
"Home at Last" (poem), 100
homelands, xvi, 16, 32, 34–37, 42, 57, 165; contrasted with property, 74–75; Hau'ofa's, ix–x, xi, 76–77
Hooper, Tony, 145
humour and laughter, 6–7, 107, 140–141, 143, 148, 150

identity. *See* regional identity
imperialism, 8, 33–35, 62–63, 75, 168
Indo-Fijian people, 14, 15, 35, 50, 148
"In Transit" (poem), 104–105
Island Boy, 60

Jahoda, Gustav, 5
Jean-Marie Tjibaou Centre, 87
Johnston Island, 49

Kame'elehiwa, Lilikalā, 66
Kelly, Walt, 99, 147
Kiribati, 11, 15, 16, 18, 33, 35, 37, 73, 77n.2
Kisses in the Nederends: extracts from, 120–135; interview with Subramani, 136–153
Koori, 75
Kundera, Milan, 69

land: relationships with, xx, 57–58, 72–75; rights and struggles over, 54, 162; as "a sea of islands," 31–32; Tongan chiefs controlling, 160, 163–164
landscapes and seascapes, 66, 72–75, 77
languages. *See* English language; French language; Pacific languages
laughter, 99, 139–141
Law of the Sea Convention, 54–55
Lawrence, Peter, 8
Lila, 60
Lini, Walter, 28

Machiavelli, 70
Māhina, 'Okusitino, 64, 72
Malinowski, Bronisław, xv, 4
Maori people, 4, 50, 70, 71, 72, 75
Mara, Ratu Sir Kamisse, 18–19
Marshall Islands, 31. *See also* Bikini Atoll
Marxism and neo-Marxism, 44, 47, 62, 166
McNamara, Josaia: *Dusia na yalo dina* (painting), 1; *Noqu Kalou noqu vanua* (painting), 155
Mead, Margaret, 7–8
Mekeo, Inequality and Ambivalence in a Village Society, xi, 103–104
Mekeo people, xi, 73–74, 104
Melanesia, 19, 29, 33, 40n.3. *See also* Melanesian people
Melanesian people, 5–7, 16, 28, 33
memories, 9, 67, 69–71, 73, 76–77
Michener, James, 45
Micronesia, 29–30, 34, 40n.3
Miller, James, 75
Mishra, Sudesh, 60

missionaries, 6, 28, 63, 165, 177. *See also* Christianity
Moruroa Atoll, 49

Naikece, Mili, 83
Naipaul, V. S., xi, 99
Narokobi, Bernard, 28
Native Land and Foreign Desires, 66
Nayacakalou, Rusiate, 8
neocolonialism: dependency in, 38, 41, 47; general process of, 30, 33, 62, 168
New Caledonia, 11, 19, 33, 77n.2, 87. *See also* New Caledonian people
New Caledonian people, 16, 50
New Zealand: immigration to, 34, 36, 41, 50, 81, 165; influencing Oceania's educational systems, 14, 89, 91, 176; as regional center, xii, 8, 10–23, 32, 45; in South Pacific Forum, 12, 48–49. *See also* Aotearoa; Maori people
Niue, 14, 15, 33, 35, 77n.2

Oceania: arts and creativity in, 80–93; Central, East, and West, 66, 70, 77n.2; common culture and heritage of, 52–58; defined, 32; history of, 60–79; Project New Oceania, xiv–xx; regional identity of, 37, 41–59, 86; as sea of islands, 27–40; values, x
Oceania Centre for Arts and Culture, ix, xvi–xx, 51–52, 56–57, 83–93
Oceania Dance Theatre, 91
ocean resources, 37–38, 42, 49–50, 55, 57, 144
Ohele, Kalani, 72
oral narratives and tradition: historiography of, 64; history contained in, 33–34, 61, 63; in landscapes, 66, 72–73, 75; nonacademic writing, use in, 108–109; perspective on Oceania, 31, 64, 70
Our Crowded Islands, 103, 108, 144
"Our Fathers Bent the Winds" (poem), 105–106

Pacific Islands region, 11, 18–21, 32, 41, 45–58. *See also* Oceania
Pacific languages: belittlement with, 28; landscapes and non-linearity in, 66–67, 73–74; lingua francas in, 33; profanities and obscenities in, 147–148; researchers use of, 7–9; suppression of, 70–71
Pacific Studies, x, 44, 51
Pacific Way, 17, 43–44, 50, 150
Papua New Guinea, 6–7, 15, 19, 28, 68, 81; Hau'ofa's life and research in, x, xiv–xvii, 44, 62, 98–99, 140–141, 151; regional associations with, 11, 16. *See also* Mekeo people
peasants and peasantry, 27, 76, 149–150, 162. *See also* class; poor people
Polynesia, 28, 29, 30–31, 40n.3. *See also* Polynesian people
Polynesian Cultural Center, xvi, 81
Polynesian people: compared to Melanesian people, 5–6, 28; migrations of, xiv–xvi, 15–16, 22, 34–35; traditions of, 23
poor people, 11–16, 21–23, 65, 98, 164. *See also* class; peasants and peasantry
population migration and movement, 16–17, 29, 36–37, 41; as historical practice, 30, 33, 72–73. *See also* diaspora; Polynesian people, migrations of
Pule, John, 87, 90

Red Wave Collective, xviii, xix, 87
regional identity, xix, 17, 41–59, 86–87. *See also* Oceania; Pacific Way
regional integration, 11–13, 15–18, 144. *See also* regional identity
religion, xix, 99–100, 150, 152, 157. *See also* Christianity; missionaries
remittances, 29, 36, 164
resistance, 39, 71, 76; to external domination, 63, 65, 75–76; to external funding, 91–92; in Tonga, 158, 167
Rotuma, 33

Sahlins, Marshall, xiii, 5
Said, Edward, xi
Sālote, Queen, 172–173, 174
Samoa: aristocracy and chiefs, 33, 159, 161, 165, 167; language of, 7–8, 71; regional association, 77n.2; resources, 35. *See also* Samoan people; Western Samoa
Samoan people, xiv, 33, 50–51, 81
Sevele, Feleti, 178
Sexual Life of Savages, The, 5
Social Organization of Manu'a, 7–8
Solomon Island people, 81, 92
Solomon Islands, x, 16, 33, 77n.2. *See also* Solomon Island people
South Pacific Conference, 45, 47–48
South Pacific Forum, 12, 45, 48
South Pacific region, 11–23, 45, 47, 49, 144, 151. *See also* Oceania; regional identity
Subramani, 136–153

Tales of the South Pacific, 45
Tales of the Tikongs, xiii, 107–109, 143, 147, 148; extract from, 110–119
Tāufa'āhau Tupou IV (King), 19, 172–179
Teaiwa, Teresia, 41
technology, 36, 68–69, 72, 76, 88
Thaggard, Lillian, 83
time, conceptions of, 62, 64–68, 73
Tokelau, 15, 33, 35, 51, 77n.2
Tonga: aristocracy and chiefs, 28, 33–34, 76, 157–171; churches and religion, 157, 166–167, 175–176; commoners in, 28, 101, 158–169, 176–178; democratisation of, 157–171; educational system of, 14, 165–166, 176–177; humour, 140–141; influence on Hau'ofa, xi, xiii, xiv–xv, 97–106, 144; land tenure system, 163–164; monarchy, 157–159, 164, 166–167, 175–178; primogeniture succession, 161; societal flexibility, 152; three pillars of society, 175–179. *See also* Tāufa'āhau Tupou IV (King); Tongan language and proverbs; Tongan people
Tongan language and proverbs, 28, 32, 66–67, 71, 73–74, 101
Tongan people, 3, 32, 50, 81, 140–141, 148
Tora, Sailasa, 91
tourism, 17, 44, 81–82
Trask, Haunani-Kay, 61
tree and canoe, 81
Tungī. *See* Tāufa'āhau Tupou IV (King)
Tupou III. *See* Sālote, Queen
Tupou IV. *See* Tāufa'āhau Tupou IV (King)
Tupou College, 175–177
Tuvalu, 16, 33, 35, 51, 77n.2

University of Papua New Guinea, xvi, 3–4
University of the South Pacific: and development, xii, 15; and globalisa-

tion, 80–91; group identities at, 50–51; Hau'ofa's role at, xi–xii, xvi, 101, 102; as regional center, xix, 15, 37, 43–44
Uvea (Wallis), xiv, 33, 77n.2

Vanuatu, x, 28, 33, 47, 51, 77n.2, 81

Waddell, Eric, 71
Walcott, Derek, 54
Walker, Geoff, 142
Wansolwara, 52
Wendt, Albert, 56, 152
Western Samoa, 14, 15, 19, 48, 50, 77n.2. *See also* Samoa
working class. *See* class; peasants and peasantry; poor people
writing, academic and nonacademic, 107–109

About the Author

Of Tongan parentage, Epeli Hau'ofa was born in 1939 in Papua New Guinea. He went to school in Papua New Guinea, Tonga, Fiji, and Australia and to universities in Australia and Canada. His first postgraduate field research was conducted in Trinidad, where he discovered V. S. Naipaul, whose early novels have had a lasting impact on him.

Since 1983 he has been working at the University of the South Pacific's main campus in Suva, Fiji. He is the founder and current director of the Oceania Centre for Arts and Culture. His work for the largest Pacific Islands regional organization has taken him several times to all the twelve countries that own the USP except the remote and nearly inaccessible Tokelau.

He and his wife, Barbara, live on a small farm in the forests outside Suva, where they breathe lots of fresh air and drink unlimited supplies of natural, unbottled Fiji water.

Production Notes for *Hau'ofa / We Are the Ocean: Selected Works*

Designed by University of Hawai'i Press production staff with text and display in Garamond and Garamond Three

Composition by Josie Herr

Printed on 55# House Natural Hi-Bulk, 360 ppi